THE POTTED
GARDEN

New Plants and New Approaches
for Container Gardens

Scott D. Appell, Editor

FOR THE
ADVANCE
MENT OF
BOTANY
AND THE
SERVICE OF
THE CITY

BROOKLYN
BOTANIC
GARDEN
PUBLICATIONS
· MMI ·

Janet Marinelli
SERIES EDITOR

Sigrun Wolff Saphire
ASSOCIATE EDITOR

Mark Tebbitt
SCIENCE EDITOR

Anne Garland
ART DIRECTOR

Steven Clemants
VICE-PRESIDENT, SCIENCE & PUBLICATIONS

Judith D. Zuk
PRESIDENT

Elizabeth Scholtz
DIRECTOR EMERITUS

Handbook #168
Copyright © 2001 by the Brooklyn Botanic Garden, Inc.
Handbooks in the *21st-Century Gardening Series,* formerly *Plants & Gardens,*
are published quarterly at 1000 Washington Ave., Brooklyn, NY 11225.
Subscription included in Brooklyn Botanic Garden subscriber membership dues ($35.00 per year).
ISBN # 1-889538-22-1
Printed by Science Press, a division of the Mack Printing Group.
Printed on recycled paper.

TABLE OF CONTENTS

INTRODUCTION

THE POTTED GARDEN

SCOTT D. APPELL

GROWING PLANTS IN CONTAINED SOIL is nothing new. In fact, the practice has a long and remarkable history. Carved scenes on the limestone walls of an Egyptian temple at Deir el-Bahri, which date back 3500 years to the dynasty of Queen Hatshepsut, depict frankincense trees growing in pots. The famed Hanging Gardens of Babylon were built under King Nebuchadnezzar II, who ruled Babylon (near modern-day Baghdad) in the 6th century BC. These immense rooftop gardens (installed for one of his wives, who was homesick for Persia) were so large that the paths within them could accommodate two chariots passing each other. The ancient Romans grew shrubs, vines, flowering plants, and even trees in containers placed on balconies, window ledges, and rooftops, as portrayed in their frescoes.

For 21st-century horticulturists, containers are truly integral to the art of gardening. Many devoted urbanites do not have access to a garden space at all, and rely solely on containers in a rooftop, terrace, or balcony setting. (Remember that fire escape gardening is illegal—*I know* from personal experience!) Suburban or rural dwellers, who may have some outdoor garden space, may enlarge

Opposite and right: Potted plants providing a profusion of blooms all summer long.

5

their plant collection—and beautify their surroundings—with containers stationed on patios, decks, allées, or lawns. And as far as I'm concerned, every window should be fitted with a beautifully planted window box, and every eave should hold a hanging basket!

The choice of containers is as unlimited as the plant material cultivated inside them. The receptacle may be an aged, algae-covered terra-cotta favorite, an upscale custom-built teak planter box, a rare antique delftware umbrella stand, a leaky half whiskey barrel, or a whimsical, white-washed ceramic wishing well, to name just a few possibilities. In addition, breakthroughs in design and manufacturing techniques of recycled plastic and fiberglass have given gardeners containers that are decorative and lightweight as well as winter-resistant, which makes them suitable for year-round use in colder climates—no more fine imported terra-cotta cracked through winter freezes. Improved styles of hanging baskets and window boxes promote better plant health, and cutting-edge soil mixes and timed watering devices save the busy container gardener precious time.

As far as plant material is concerned, gardeners can choose from a seemingly inexhaustible array of newly introduced varieties: drought-resistant and cold-hardy species, pollution- and disease-resistant strains, and miniature selections for limited spaces are merely a few examples.

So whether you cultivate a vast patio landscape, a small veranda planting, a miniature alpine garden, a luxurious water garden in a tub, a strawberry jar brimming with herbs, or simply a coveted, solitary pot of geraniums, rejoice in container gardening!

Pick a container and start a potted garden wherever you find some outdoor space.

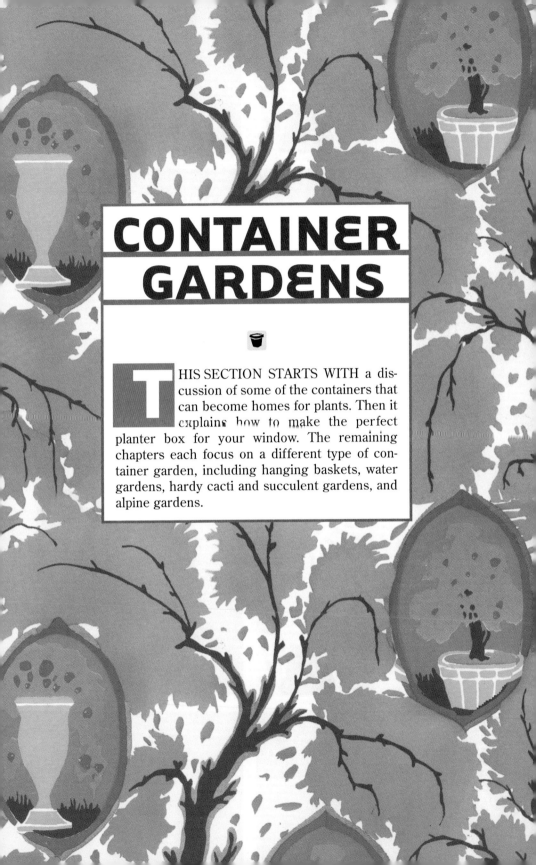

CONTAINER GARDENS

THIS SECTION STARTS WITH a discussion of some of the containers that can become homes for plants. Then it explains how to make the perfect planter box for your window. The remaining chapters each focus on a different type of container garden, including hanging baskets, water gardens, hardy cacti and succulent gardens, and alpine gardens.

UNUSUAL, ANTIQUE, AND COLLECTABLE CONTAINERS

SCOTT D. APPELL

ANYTHING THAT CAN HOLD SOIL can serve as a home for plants—which expands the selection into realms far beyond the standard terra-cotta flowerpot or ubiquitous plastic window box. Choose from a vast array of traditional, innovative, daring, whimsical, or intriguing designs ranging from lucky flea market finds to costly antiques: a discarded wicker basket, a strawberry jar, a coal bucket with a new lease on life, a leaky soup tureen, a milk crate, a footed lead urn, an authentic

Ming vessel, or a Victorian chimney pot.

A potted planting begins with the container. The container you select is as important to the overall design scheme as the plants you decide to grow in it. Delicate antique ceramic and porce-

Opposite and above: The choice of containers is as unlimited as the plants cultivated within them. Antique lead cisterns and flue tiles are two options.

lain finds (minton ware, McCoy, and majolica, for example), and jardinières, arborettes, jardinets, and cachepots make wonderfully unique planters—especially when they are overflowing with your favorite annuals and herbs. However, their fragility and expense warrants a sheltered (wind-free) spot in the garden during the summer, and, in colder climates, a frost-free spot for the winter, where they can await the next growing season emptied of plant material and soil.

STRAWBERRY JARS

Particularly favored by Victorian gardeners, the aptly named containers with the bulbous planter-pockets were popular for cultivating strawberries. Planted in the mouth at the top, strawberry plants put out stolons and form new plants that can be trained to fill the pockets below. Another familiar picture is a planting of hens and chicks (*Sempervivum* species), filling the pockets and creeping happily over the bare external surface of the pot. Strawberry jars are available in a variety of materials: terra-cotta, concrete, wood, and fine ceramic, including blue-decorat-

Moisture-loving plants like these *Cyperus* find a perfect home in glazed ceramic containers that lack drainage holes.

ed delftware. (You can also make your own by cutting planter holes into the sides of a staved barrel, using a door lock drill bit.) Their low center of gravity makes strawberry jars practically "tumble-free" in windstorms, but it pays to be extra careful when siting fine ceramic specimens.

JARDINIÈRES AND CACHEPOTS

The difference between jardinière and cachepot is a matter of size: Generally speaking, jardinières are wider than eight inches at the mouth. These 19th-century glazed ceramic favorites were designed as pot covers; planted clay pots would be slipped into the confines of the jardinière or cachepot. Intended as attractive time-saving devices, they made the horticultural housekeeping chore of scrubbing off the soluble salts, algae, and molds from the exterior surfaces of earthenware flowerpots superfluous. Plastic had not yet been invented!

There are several ways to use jardinières and cachepots for modern container gardens. You can slip flower- or herb-filled plastic or clay pots into them, but the lack of drainage holes is a serious disadvantage. To keep the jardinière or cachepot from flooding every time you water the plant, you really should remove the inserted pot, water the plant, let it drain, and replace the pot. If that sounds too time-consuming, you might consider drilling drainage holes in the bottom of the piece, using a carbide-tipped concrete or porcelain drill bit (readily available at hardware stores). The jardinière or cachepot now functions in the same way as any freely draining decorative container. Another option for the clever gardener is to use the lack of drainage as an asset and cultivate moisture-loving plants like

PLANTING A
STRAWBERRY JAR

Due to their unique shape, strawberry jars require a special planting technique. Inevitably, in the center of the jar there is a shaft of poorly drained, root-free soil that remains damp at all times, allowing the spread of fungal pathogens, which lead to root rot. To avoid the problem, you need to install a drainage column made up of a mixture of pea gravel (tiny pebbles) and horticultural charcoal (there is no exact recipe; a mixture of approximately one part charcoal to nine parts gravel works well). The important tool for this procedure is a tube that is long enough to reach from the mouth of the jar all the way to the bottom. For example, a cardboard toilet paper tube may be just the right height for a tiny porcelain strawberry jar; a cardboard paper towel tube may work for a pot of medium height; and a length of plastic pipe (from the local hardware store) can be cut to fit any large-size container.

Installation is simple, though an extra set of hands may be helpful—especially for large pots: Center and stand the empty tube upright inside the strawberry jar (the extra set of hands can hold the tube in place). Place a shallow layer of the pea gravel and charcoal mixture at the bottom of the pot surrounding the tube. Fill the tube with the pea gravel mixture as well. Then begin to fill the jar with potting soil and plant the pockets starting with the lowest, and work upwards to several inches below the rim of the jar. Gently give the strawberry jar a sharp rap on the potting table to settle the soil. Carefully remove the tube from the soil, leaving the vertical column of pea gravel and charcoal behind. Finally, plant in the open mouth of the jar, then water.

11

papyrus (*Cyperus papyrus*), calamus (*Acorus calamus*), and umbrella plant (*Cyperus alternifolius*). Or perhaps use a large jardinière for a miniature water garden.

ARBORETTES AND JARDINETS

Jardinets are glazed ceramic pieces designed to look like small (eight to 18 inches tall), moss-covered, hollow tree stumps. Much taller, and made of molded terra-cotta, arborettes are far more elaborate tree-like structures with multiple branches that end in planting holes. They are marvelous to behold and quite collectable. Try placing them where their unusual features can be appreciated: at, or just below, eye level works best. Originally designed to hold forced spring-flowering bulbs, arborettes and jardinets are useful outdoors, as well. Plant them with delicate ferns (*Adiantum* or *Pteris* species) and set them on a shady garden table, or with lobelia (*Lobelia* species) or creeping zinnia (*Sanvitalia procumbens*) in a sunny nook on an étagère. In areas with cold winters, these unique containers should be brought indoors at the end of the gardening season.

TROUGHS

Trough gardens aren't all that unusual, but how about making your own? Give homemade samples an artistic edge by using uncommonly shaped plastic containers as the initial mold. To achieve a tall, narrow trough, mold "hypertufa" mix (see "Water Gardens in Small Containers," page 34, for instructions) over a plastic water bottle with the narrow neck removed. For a squat trough, take an empty gallon milk jug, also with the top and handle removed. Before planting, make sure to drill drainage holes in the bottom of your homemade trough.

BASKETS

Baskets are by far the most beloved and familiar containers for planting. Whether they are recycled curios, garage sale gems, or newly requisitioned dime store finds, they make decorative containers thanks to their natural coloration and interesting textures—which offset the flowers and foliage of innumerable plants. The more a basket is protected from the elements and from the harmful effects of frequent watering, the longer it will last. So, it's a good idea to treat valuable and collectable basketware with a varnish, polyurethane, or some other protective coating. To prevent major soil leakage and root exposure, you need to line the basket before planting, a simple task requiring sheet moss (from a florist supply house), sturdy clear or black sheet plastic (from a hardware store), and potting soil. First line the selected basket with the moss, decorative side out. Spread the plastic sheeting over the moss, making sure to punch drainage holes at regular intervals using an ice pick or other pointy tool. Fill the lined basket with soil and plant in the usual fashion. To prolong the life of the basket, remove the liner at the end of the gardening season, empty out the soil, and store the basket in a cool, dry place for the winter.

BUILDING WINDOW AND PLANTER BOXES

BILL SHANK

THE FIRST IMPORTANT POINT TO CONSIDER when making a window or planter box is that the finished planter should complement the style of its surroundings. A rustic stone container will probably not look its best if it is set against a Colonial revival building; nor will a classical design necessarily work well in a contemporary setting. So, think about colors, textures, and design options before getting started. Construct your very own planter in the style and material that work in your environment.

Ideally, a container should be at least eight inches high and measure ten inches

Make your own window box in the style, material, and size that suit the location.

or more across. The length of the container is a matter of choice; just remember to size a window box so that it fits snugly on the window ledge. If you're building a planter for a very long ledge, one box may be too unwieldy to maneuver; try making several instead and place them end to end. Always make sure that the window ledge can safely support the added weight and that the box is securely fastened to the window frame. Use screw hooks, strong wire run through holes in the box, or a chain attached to screw eyes fastened to the window frame, especially if you are placing the box in a window that's above ground floor. Never underestimate the weight of a full, exuberantly planted window box with wet soil.

BUILDING A RUSTIC PLANTER BOX

Bluestone pavers sold for patio use, slate or marble panels, and inexpensive concrete pavers can be transformed into a rustic planter box (see illustration on this page). A container made of pavers is rather heavy, so if you intend to use it as a window box, choose a window that's not too large. A small window in an old stone cottage is the perfect place.

Figure out the dimensions of your planter before heading to the local stoneyard, so you can have the panels cut to size right there. You need to have five pieces in all: two end pieces that are at least eight inches high and ten inches wide; two pieces for the front and back panels that are the same height as the end pieces and the desired width of the container minus two times the thickness of an end piece; and one piece cut to fit inside the bottom of the box. Then have the stoneyard drill four holes in each piece, one in every corner, set in two inches from the edges in both directions.

Fasten all of the pieces together with at least two loops of heavy-gauge wire. Thread the wire through the adjacent holes in each corner and twist-tie them on the inside of the box. Make sure the panels are close together and make a sturdy box. You can further secure the pavers by running a line of aquarium silicone glue carefully along the inside seams, taking care that it doesn't show on the outside of the box. Be sure to leave gaps in the silicone seal along the bottom seams for drainage, or have holes drilled into the bottom panel.

Once the box is ready, put it in place and line the inside with window screen or landscape fabric. The liner will allow drainage of excess water through the seams between the pavers and will also keep the potting soil from leaking out.

BUILDING A RUSTIC PLANTER BOX—Panels of bluestone, marble, or concrete are cut to measure and joined with heavy-gauge wire for an attractive, durable planter.

Fill the planter with your favorite soil mix and install plants that will grow well in the light available at the site. In front of a sunny window, this type of box makes an excellent environment for herbs, but it also works well as a free-standing container in the herb garden or other location. Succulents also look beautiful in this rather rustic-looking container.

CONSTRUCTING A SUMMER HOME FOR HOUSEPLANTS

We all look forward to our summer vacations, and your houseplants would love to have one, too. All your indoor plants are candidates for spending the summer outdoors. One way to give them a restorative vacation is to place the pots outside your window into a conventional window box surrounded with growing medium. But, why not fit the outside of your window with a custom-made plant shelf that can hold your favorite houseplants in their own pots and matches the the architecture of your home? This set-up is ideal for a north-facing window or one in deep shade.

The basic element of the structure is a ¾-inch waterproof plywood panel that fits on your window ledge (see illustrations on this page). Before installing the plywood panel, cut holes in it for the individual pots; this will allow water drain-

BUILDING A SUMMER HOME FOR HOUSE-PLANTS—A plywood panel cut with holes to hold individual plants is fastened to a window ledge (below) and fitted with a decorative panel on the outside (right).

ing from the pots to run off freely. Then fasten the panel to the base of the ledge with screw hooks and eyes like those used for wooden window screens. This will keep the panel from sliding off the ledge. Fasten large screw hooks into the window frame (on the outside) at the height where the top and bottom sashes meet. Be careful not to obstruct the working of the sashes.

A heavy chain carries the weight of the plant shelf. Run the chain between the two large hooks on either side of the window sash and secure it to large hooks that you install with a large washer and nut under the two outside corners of the shelf panel. Adjust the length of the chain to keep the panel slightly tilting away from the window. This prevents excess water from watering or rain from backing up against the window.

Always make sure the window ledge can safely support the added weight of a window box and that the box is securely fastened.

Arrange the containers on the shelf in any way you like; for example, repeat a favorite indoor tropical grouping outdoors. But be mindful of the overall weight of the plant shelf and be careful not to make so many holes so close together that the plywood panel is weakened. Place heavier pots closer to the window ledge and lighter ones farther out.

Once you have assembled the basic shelf, you can fit the outside with decorative panels that match or complement the architectural style of your home. The panels are made of the same ¾-inch waterproof plywood and can be cut with a scroll saw and painted, or covered with classic moldings, pickets, or even small branches.

You can also adapt this type of shelf to make a free-standing table for a shady location in your yard. Another adaptation of this idea is to construct a shelf or tiers of shelves around the base of a tree.

Remember, your houseplants will enjoy a summer sitting outdoors in the filtered light and fresh air as much as you do.

FORMAL ARRANGEMENTS IN CLASSIC CONTAINERS

RICHARD R. IVERSEN

I AM FOND OF CONTAINERS fashioned in the classic style—those that imitate the form and proportion of an ancient Grecian or Roman vase. Since Renaissance times these classic containers have been used as garden ornaments to delight and amuse. A Grecian vase probably dating from the 1st century AD first appeared in the inventory of the Villa Medici in Rome in 1598 and a similar vase was known to be in the Villa Borghese, also in Rome, in 1645. Marble Grecian-style vases were used by André Le Nôtre when he designed the gardens at Vaux-le-Vicomte and Versailles in the 17th century.

Since Le Nôtre copied the Grecian vase, the style has been in continuous manufacture in an infinite variety of sizes and materials, including stone, terra-cotta, poured concrete, bronze, cast iron, silver, porcelain, glass, plastic, and fiberglass. They have been used to embellish the architecture of buildings and to decorate interior rooms and outdoor spaces.

America's first professional landscape gardener, Andrew Jackson Downing, advocated the use of decorative vases to create a "union between the house and garden." In order to provide a gradual transition from the architecture of the building to the surrounding grounds, Downing positioned vases around the house along terrace balustrades or within flower gardens, in places where they could be seen from inside. He also placed them beyond the terrace onto the lawn, but always near the house. Downing maintained that "so artificial and architectural an object as a sculptured vase, is never correctly introduced unless it appears someway connected with buildings or objects of a like architectural character." This harmony of form was often lost when classic-style vases were contrasted with natural objects, such as overhanging trees in informal settings.

Grecian- and Roman-style vases have been used in gardens since the 17th century.

Grecian vases are the proper appendage to formal gardens, large or small. Positioned in harmony with the symmetry of the borders or beds, they strengthen the geometric design. For example, try placing four vases at the junctions of four corners. Or use containers to direct the flow of traffic where pathways intersect.

To highlight the entry to a house favoring symmetry—one in the Georgian or Federal style—I like to place a pair of classic containers on both sides of the main doorway. A pair of vases is also useful to define the beginning of a pathway; a single vase may signal the end of a path by becoming its focal point. Positioned in the center of a circular flower bed where brightly colored annual or bedding plants are massed, a vase will elevate and accentuate the arrangement.

No matter where you position a Grecian-style container, it needs a firm base or pedestal. Without a base, the container looks temporary and meek. However, placed on a plinth, it becomes transformed: stable and dignified. The pedestal may be manufactured of the same material as the container or made from a block of stone or a column of bricks.

PLANTING A CLASSIC CONTAINER

Artfully shaped vases used as architectural elements are beautiful even without plants growing inside them. In fact, some plants may clash with vases, reducing them to flowerpots. When plants are installed, they should have strong architectural habits.

Plants with a geometric branching habit and an unbending form that's stiff as

A classic vase looks best when it's set atop a firm base or pedestal.

steel can be very powerful accent specimens. Like crisply carved marble in a museum courtyard, they make a strong visual impact. For the most sculptural effect, plant a single architectural plant in the center of a Grecian vase atop a pedestal.

Among the best examples of architectural plants are those within the agave family (Agavacoae). The leaves of these plants are as strong as their stems, creating a forceful form that boldly stands out among other plants. These rigid specimens provide as sculptured an effect as the Grecian vases they're planted in.

Most plants in this family possess long and linear, spear-shaped leaves with veins running parallel to each other. Common genera include *Agave, Furcraea, Yucca, Cordyline, Phormium, Dracaena,* and *Sansevieria.* Most are tender tropical or subtropical plants that will not tolerate freezing temperatures. To keep these tender plants alive in colder climates you need to overwinter them in a frost-free environment, such as a garage, basement, or sunroom, or on a windowsill.

Containers with wide diameters, generally greater than twelve inches, can support several kinds of tender plants. In my mind, classicism and symmetry are synonymous, so when I do install plants in classic-style containers, I arrange them in a symmetric pattern that fans out from the center. Floral and foliage colors, textures, and forms can either blend or contrast.

Into the center of the container (sometimes called a "tazza") plant one tall and upright architectural plant, like *Cordyline indivisa* (cabbage tree) or *Yucca.* These plants were often used as the center spike of a tazza during the late 19th century. See "Architectural Plants for Classic Containers," page 21 for details. Surround

Ornamental pineapples like *Ananas comosus* 'Variegatus', above, are a good choice for the center of a classic container.

the center plant with short, full plants that slope outward and downward, such as the mounding bedding plants *Alternanthera ficoidea* (Joseph's coat), *Begonia* Semperflorens-cultorum Group (wax begonia), or coleus. Finally, add prostrate plants that will cascade over the edge, such as nasturtiums or inch plants, around the rim. Grown outdoors, *Tradescantia zebrina* (inch plant or wandering jew) is dense and vibrant, not spindly and dusty as it inevitably becomes when grown indoors. The succulent stems mat together, hiding the soil, then drape down the sides of the container. Flat leaves, about one inch wide and two inches long, are striped with two silver bands. Upper leaf surfaces shimmer like steel; undersurfaces are darker-colored, like a concord grape. Sunlight stimulates purple pigment production and intensifies the leaf color. Best of all, these plants are determined to grow. Failure with them is nearly impossible. They flourish in the damp shade, but should they wander into full sunshine, they look even better.

Plants in the genera *Agave*, *Furcraea*, and *Yucca* are desert dwellers that survive drought conditions in barren soil and full sunshine, so they require little water and are easy to maintain. As a result, they are good candidates for Grecian-style vases that have a narrow diameter and a relatively small planting space, which may dry out quickly. They tolerate a lot of neglect, but will reward good cultivation—full sunshine, proper growing mix, normal water, fast drainage, and any general foliage-plant fertilizer—with speedy growth.

Pineapples are also good candidates for the center stage of a Grecian-style vase. They have strong, symmetric outlines. Long (about three feet), serrated leaves whorl from the heart of the plant and cascade over the container's edge.

Screw pines (*Pandanus* species) are as architectural as agaves or pineapples. *Pandanus* is a genus of ornamental trees and large shrubs native to tropical regions of Asia, Africa, and Australia.

ARCHITECTURAL PLANTS
FOR CLASSIC CONTAINERS

CENTURY PLANT *Agave americana*—This bold and brassy Mexican succulent is the classic architectural plant recommended for use in sculptured vases. (The English horticulturist John Claudius Loudon advocated its use in 1833.) From the muscular heart of the American aloe, which is its other common name, emerge thick and leathery leaves, 3 to 6 feet long, that twist, snake, and finally cascade down the sides of the container. The familiar color is silvery blue-green, but leaves of the cultivar *Agave americana* 'Marginata' sport yellow margins, and those of *Agave americana* 'Mediopicta' have yellow centers. Spines, which can rip your skin like a knife, line the edges of all *Agave americana* leaves and a dangerous stiff needle protrudes from the leaf apex. Set the vase on top of a tall plinth so the agave leaves are above eye level. In public spaces or anywhere children run, it's crucial to place these plants very carefully.

The common name century plant refers to its reputed habit of flowering only once in a century. However, when given favorable growing conditions, amazing flower stalks reaching 20 feet in height can emerge in fewer than ten years. Should your agave flower, be pleasantly surprised, but don't expect it. After the event, the plant begins to die, as a profusion of "pups" (juvenile plants) form at its base to ensure continuity.

MAURITIUS HEMP *Furcraea foetida* 'Mediopicta'—This succulent, agave-like, but with fewer spines, is special. From the center of the plant emerge upright, rigid leaves that are about 5 inches wide and 3 feet long. Ice cream color stripes of French vanilla and mint-green illuminate them. As new leaves form, older ones spiral downward until they rest on the soil surface, yielding a spherical silhouette. They may then act as tubs and collect water where small golden warblers are known to bathe.

SPINELESS YUCCA *Yucca guatemalensis* (*elephantipes*)—This tender yucca begins its life as a groundcover rosette of sword-shaped leaves, about 1 to 4 feet long. In some cultivars they are bordered with creamy white stripes; in others a central golden stripe develops. As the plant matures, the foliage crown rises atop a straight trunk several feet tall. Plants thrive in full sun with normal irrigation, but tolerate lots of neglect.

CABBAGE TREE *Cordyline indivisa*—The center stem of this plant is vertical, but like *Furcraea* and *Yucca*, the overall outline formed by the firm, linear leaves that spiral around it is spherical. It is one of the most common architectural plants. Ease of cultivation contributed to its popularity a century ago, when it was frequently planted in vases with red geraniums and variegated vinca. As an unbranched spike, 2 feet to 6 feet tall, *Cordyline*

Cabbage tree is a common architectural plant.

indivisa (sometimes called *Dracaena indivisa*) acts as the sentinel of the space it occupies, connecting soil and sky. Long, lance-shaped leaves whorl around a stiff stem with symmetric balance. A similar plant, *Cordyline australis* 'Purpurea', combines burgundy-colored leaves with this strong shape. The richest shade of burgundy occurs when plants grow in full sunshine.

NEW ZEALAND FLAX

Phormium tenax—Unlike *Cordyline indivisa,* New Zealand flax doesn't produce a central trunk, but its effect in the garden is similar. Sword-shaped linear leaves, 3 to 6 feet long, form a vertical accent to punctuate plantings. Magnificent bronze, variegated, or waxy green, iris-like, flat foliar fans develop from a rhizome beneath the soil. The best New Zealand flax plants are older than one year, so try to overwinter them. It's easy. Before the first frost, dig, pot, and bring plants into a frost-free garage or basement, or put them on a windowsill with some light. *Phormium* tolerates and prefers cold winter temperatures, but not frost. Water monthly. Acclimate plants to full sunshine in spring, and when nighttime temperatures are above 50° F., plant them outdoors in enriched soil. For a convincing specimen look, don't divide plants until they're three years old.

SNAKE PLANT *Sansevieria trifasciata*—Few herbaceous plants are as tough as the species and cultivars of the common houseplant *Sansevieria trifasciata*, also known as mother-in-law's tongue. They grow anywhere in anything, in full sun or light shade. Cultivated as outdoor container centerpieces, they lose their common houseplant association and become a strong vertical element in the outdoor environment.

PINEAPPLE *Ananas* species —As tempted as you may be, don't grow the heads of grocery store pineapples. The ornamental cultivars, *Ananas comosus* 'Variegatus' or *Ananas bracteatus* 'Tricolor', are grown not for their fruit but rather for the cream and pink stripes that ribbon down the length of their leaves, making them look like candy. These delicious leaves are more beautiful and last longer than fruits. Visually, variegated pineapple plants are like tigers: they pounce at you. Use them where you

New Zealand flax is a good vertical accent plant.

need a strong focal point, either in full sun or part shade.

SCREW PINE *Pandanus* species—The 3- to 5-foot long linear leaves of screw pines are spear-like, similar to a pineapple leaf. On some species, the leaf edge is spiny, and the leaf is truly like a spear. Don't let that dissuade you from growing it, however. The leaf arrangement, overlapping at the base then spiraling around the stem, makes for a plant of extraordinary architecture. After the leaves fall, the scars resemble the threads of a screw, contributing to its common name. In some species the leaves are striped—either white, as in *Pandanus veitchii*, or gold, as in *Pandanus baptistii* 'Aureus'. Just as remarkable as the foliage are the thick, aerial prop roots that project from the side of the stem at an angle, grow downward, and enter the soil to support the plant. Plants grow in full sun and moist conditions but acclimate to shade and tolerate some drought.

HANGING GARDENS

ELLEN ZACHOS

YOUR GARDEN IS BEAUTIFULLY LANDSCAPED, but when you look at your house, something seems to be missing. Did you forget to accessorize? With hanging containers you can place spots of color exactly where you want them. They're like jewelry for your home; without them your house is only half-dressed.

Hanging planters have appealed to gardeners for centuries. Until the mid-1800s, hanging containers were made of metal. They were heavy, expensive, and affordable only for princes or those with princely incomes. In the mid-19th century, the entrepreneur Henry Bessemer developed a method for manufacturing durable, lightweight wire—a material that proved ideal for hanging baskets, often available in elaborate designs. When galvanization was developed a few years later, the useful life of Victorian wire baskets was greatly extended and they became even more popular. (Today's wire baskets are plastic-coated for durability and rust proofing.)

Those were the days of full-time gardeners and glasshouse conservatories, when hanging baskets were carefully groomed and maintained by staff horticulturists—at least in the homes of a lucky few. I certainly don't want to scare you off, but hanging baskets do require

Left and opposite: Hanging containers overflowing with an array of trailing and upright plants are beautiful to look at, but they do require special care.

Half-baskets look best when planted against a wall or fence.

extra care for several reasons. First, they dry out quickly, since they are exposed to the sun, wind, and cold on all sides and water evaporates not only through the soil surface but also through the sides and bottom of the basket. They are typically filled with an array of plants overflowing in every direction, with little room for soil, and consequently retain little water to begin with. Finally, since they often hang in places where they don't get any rain—under arbors and trellises, for example—baskets may depend solely on watering by hand.

CONTAINERS

Many different kinds of containers are suitable for hanging, from commercially available wire and plastic baskets to household objects that can be transformed into unique containers. Do you have an old birdcage in the attic crying out for a Boston fern? Colanders, wicker baskets, and galvanized buckets all make excellent potted gardens. There's almost no limit to what you can use as a container: if you can hang it and poke drainage holes in it, you can plant a garden in it. Just remember that even a lightweight container will be heavy when fully planted and watered. So, secure planter brackets with heavy-duty anchors and choose a strong crossbeam, if you're drilling into wood.

Different containers are best suited to different locations, sunny or shady, for example. Here are some of the commercially available options:

TERRA-COTTA POTS

If you pick a container made from a porous material like terra-cotta, try lining the pot with a thick layer of newspaper to increase moisture retention. A terra-cotta container is an excellent choice for a shaded area where it won't dry out as quickly as it would in full sun. Also, a terra-cotta pot will be heavy, so don't use it in a spot that's extremely difficult to reach.

PLASTIC CONTAINERS

These require the least maintenance, because plastic is non-porous and water can't evaporate through the walls. The disadvantage is that you cannot plant the sides and bottom of a plastic basket, unless you drill holes that are at least one inch in diameter wherever you want a plant to poke through. Plastic containers are a good choice for a full-sun location, and their lighter weight makes them appropriate for a high spot that might require a ladder for access.

WIRE BASKETS OR HAYRACKS

The trick with these containers is to use a liner to keep the soil from washing away. Ready-made liners made of coir (coconut fiber) or compressed fiber are available in various sizes. (You can make your own liner from un-milled sphagnum or sheet moss, but since sphagnum moss is harvested from bogs and is a limited resource, it might be better to use one of the alternatives.) In addition to the outer liner, you should line the wire basket with plastic on the inside to help keep moisture in the soil. You'll need to make slits for drainage through both liners when it's time to plant.

Hayracks and half baskets are best suited to outdoor walls, since they hang flat against the building. If you are planning to hang the container from an arbor, trellis, or porch, choose a round one, so you have something to look at from every angle.

ORCHID BOXES

Made from wooden slats, these containers work well if you line them in the manner described above. They are an excellent choice for a rustic setting, or any other spot where natural, unpolished materials look best. Orchid boxes are available in many sizes and are of medium weight, making them easier to hang than terra-cotta. They are very porous and will dry out quickly, requiring daily (or twice daily) watering.

PLASTIC PLANTER BAGS AND CYLINDERS

Several types of these containers specially designed for hanging gardens are available. Granny's Garden Sock is a hanging bag made of rip-stop, UV-resistant material, with pre-cut slits ready for planting. The bag is 22 inches long and has drainage holes built into its seams. Charley's Greenhouse Supply sells a 14-inch-long hanging column planter that twists apart into three sections for easy planting. It has pre-cut holes for planting all around. Both of these containers are relatively lightweight and therefore easy to place in hard-to-reach locations. They are also a good choice for full sun, since they dry out less quickly than containers made of porous materials.

POTTING MIXES

A lightweight potting mix is especially important for hanging containers. It will dry out more quickly than a heavier mix, but it is your best bet for keeping the weight of the container manageable. You might consider adding horticultural charcoal to keep the mix sweet. Charcoal is antiseptic and neutralizes potentially dangerous bacteria in the potting medium. It also absorbs acids produced by decomposing organic materials.

Hydrogel granules will significantly increase the amount of water the potting mix can retain. These water-retaining polymers hold several hundred times their weight in water (one teaspoon absorbs a quart of water) and release it gradually to the plant roots. Soak the granules first, add them to the mix, then plant as usual.

PLANTING

Once you've chosen and prepared the container, picked and readied its location, and mixed a potting medium, you're ready to plant. Logistically speaking, it's best to be able to view the container from all sides while planting. If possible, hang it at or below eye level; if not, set the container on top of a bucket to start work. If you're using a basket, begin by soaking the coir or coconut outer liner in water to make it more malleable, and pat it in place, then fit a 3- or 4-mil (milinch) sheet of plastic inside the outer liner. Trim the top of the inner liner, so the plastic doesn't show above the rim. Before adding soil, make a few small slits in the bottom of the basket through both liners to make room for small trailing plants. (The cascading effect is important for a hanging basket; save the marigolds for another place and time.) If you're planting a solid container, you can skip the steps above; instead, drill a few holes in the walls and base where you want plants to poke

Left: A basket is lined with coir and plastic sheeting to hold the soil in place. To enhance the cascading effect, make a few slits through both liners and insert small trailing plants along the sides and bottom.

Opposite: Like this orchid box, which is protected from the rain by a tree, most hanging planters rely entirely on the gardener for their watering needs.

through. Make the holes large enough to allow roots to pass through without damage; between one and one and a half inches in diameter will be adequate.

It's easiest to slip young plants with small root balls through slits or holes, so use small plugs (young plants with root balls that are about one inch in diameter) to plant the bottom and sides of the basket. Wrap each plug in a small piece of plastic or stiff paper for protection. Slip the root end in through the slit liner or hole, put the plant into position, and pull the plastic or paper through to the inside. Once you've finished planting the bottom of the container, add a layer of soil to cover the roots, then move up the sides of the bas-

ket, cutting slits and planting them as you go. If you like, you can add larger plants at the top of the basket, since you don't have to fit the root balls through small slits. Leave one inch between the top of the soil and the rim of the container, and cover the soil surface with a layer of moss or coir to act as a mulch and help the container retain moisture. Even a lightweight basket can be heavy when wet, so put the container in place before watering it. Then, soak thoroughly.

WATER AND FERTILIZER

Careful maintenance, including fertilizing, watering, and dead-heading, is the key to keeping the basket beautiful all summer long.

The volume of soil that fits inside the container determines how much water it can hold, so the smaller the container, the more frequently it will need water. Try to use hanging containers that are at least nine inches in diameter. You still may need to water them once or twice a day, depending on their exposure. In a windy or sunny spot, a basket will require water more frequently than it would in a shadier, more sheltered place. If by some chance you forget to water and the soil in your basket dries out so much that it pulls away from the container walls, soak the entire basket in a tub of water for 30 minutes. If you can't soak the basket, water it thoroughly every two hours until the potting mix has fully expanded.

Consider using a pulley device to raise and lower a heavy container for easier watering. There are self-watering containers on the market as well. These work with a water reservoir, so planting through the bottom is not an option. Instead, rely on trailing plants to disguise the sides of the container.

It's important to note that frequent watering flushes away nutrients, so you'll have to fertilize hanging baskets more often, as well. A good general rule is to fertilize once every two weeks. Choose a fertilizer with an N-P-K formula in which the middle number is higher than the other two (15-30-15, for example). This formula indicates a higher phosphate content, which boosts bloom.

PICKING PLANTS

When choosing plant material for a hanging container, remember to use plants with varying growth habits, both trailing and upright. Because hanging baskets are relatively small, limit yourself to no more than three different kinds of plants and pick colors carefully. Limited space encourages innovation as you combine masses of color and shapes in a very compact area. Two bright colors interwo-

KNOCKOUT COMBINATIONS
FOR HANGING BASKETS

Each of the following suggested plant combinations features two varieties of profusely flowering ornamentals and a beautifully trailing vine.

YELLOW OSTEOSPERMUM, LICORICE PLANT, AND LANTANA
Osteospermum hybrid, *Helichrysum petiolare,* and *Lantana camara*

ZINNIA, A VARIEGATED ENGLISH IVY, AND IVY-LEAVED GERANIUM
Zinnia angustifolia, Hedera helix cultivar, and *Pelargonium peltatum*

PURPLE HYBRID PETUNIA, INCH PLANT, COMMON GARDEN VERBENA
Petunia × *hybrida, Tradescantia zebrina,* and *Verbena* × *hybrida*

FUCHSIA 'BEACON ROSA', VARIEGATED SWEDISH IVY, AND FAN FLOWER *Fuchsia* 'Beacon Rosa', *Plectranthus forsteri* 'Marginatus', and *Scaevola aemula*

A RED REX BEGONIA, GOLDEN CREEPING JENNY, AND CHENILLE PLANT *Begonia* Rex-cultorum Group, *Lysimachia nummularia* 'Aurea', and *Acalypha hispida*

BLUE BROWALLIA, NASTURTIUM, AND A BLUE EDGING LOBELIA
Browallia speciosa, Tropaeolum majus, and *Lobelia erinus*

ven with neutral foliage work very well. The fuzzy white foliage of licorice plant (*Helichrysum petiolare*) is an excellent complement to many other plants, and its trailing growth habit is quite useful.

You may want to replace annuals when they've passed their prime to keep the container fresh. If you start the growing season with pansies surrounded by ivy, you may want to replace the pansies with species petunias in mid-June and dahlias in September. The ivy will easily make it from a late frost in spring to the first few frosts in fall.

OVERWINTERING

In general, hanging containers do not do well over a cold winter. However, if you live in Zone 8 or warmer, or if you have a greenhouse or warm garage, you might try overwintering them.

Try to be attentive to your hanging garden. A few well-planted, creative containers can perfectly accessorize the exterior of your home, and isn't that worth some conscientious maintenance?

ORNAMENTAL KALE, RUFFLE-LEAFED ENGLISH IVY, AND HEATHER
Brassica oleracea: *acephala* group, *Hedera helix*, and *Calluna vulgaris* (Try lining this fall basket with evergreen branches instead of coir or moss; they'll stay green in cold weather)

PURPLE-LEAF BASIL, LEMON THYME, AND PURPLE-LEAF SAGE
Ocimum basilicum 'Purpureum', *Thymus* × *citriodorus* 'Aureus', and *Salvia officinalis* 'Purpurascens'

Combine colors, textures, and growth habits.

DWARF CHERRY TOMATO, BASIL, CHILE PEPPER
Lycopersicon esculentum, *Ocimum basilicum*, and *Capisicum annuum* var. *annuum* Longum group

WATER GARDENS IN SMALL CONTAINERS

SCOTT D. APPELL

WATER GARDENS ARE AMONG THE MOST BELOVED garden elements, with glorious water plants (featuring seemingly endless variations of blossom and foliage) and calming, rippling water combining in perfect harmony. Sadly, many would-be water gardeners never attempt the hobby because they lack garden space. Fortunately, with careful container and plant selection, anyone can create an aesthetically pleasing water feature appropriately scaled for the allotted space—no matter how restricted it may be. The key is the size of the components. Not just the pots but also the aquatic plants have to be scaled-down, smaller varieties of the flora grown by our fortunate neighbors with large tubs or ponds. These are snug harbors, indeed.

WATERTIGHT CONTAINERS

Wooden whiskey barrels (whole, half-, or quarter-cut) are easily affordable and readily available at most garden centers and nurseries. They make appealing water features, thanks to their rustic look and neutral colors. However, I find they have considerable disadvantages: When the barrels are completely dried out (at the time of purchase, or after overwintering in an empty state), it takes the wooden slats a long time to absorb enough water to make them watertight. Daily long-term soakings with the hose may eventually moisten them up to the point where they will not leak, but this is not always the case. In addition, charcoal and other residues that have permeated the wood will often taint the water—promoting methane build-up and subsequent plant death. Pre-fabricated liners are available, but the sight of the plastic on the barrel's rim is far from elegant.

To be enchanting, a water garden doesn't have to be large. Accommodate small-sized varieties of plants in a scaled-down water garden.

Miniature lotus, *Nelumbo nucifera*, finds a comfortable home in a decorative watertight ceramic container.

There are many alternatives: If your taste leans towards Americana, experiment with salt-glazed pottery, earthenware bowls, and ceramic pickle jars—all available in a wide variety of styles and sizes. Asian markets are splendid sources for glazed ceramic ware. Consider the large pottery containers that hold 1000-year-old eggs. After their contents have sold, the five-to-ten-gallon pots can be purchased quite cheaply from Chinese groceries. The surface design of these containers ranges from simple unadorned beige to highly ornamental patterns, often with lotus and goldfish motifs. In fact, the sundry shops in Asian neighborhoods are fabulous locales to procure beautifully glazed jardinières, footed urns, bowls, tureens, and other vessels of every imaginable size, shape, and color.

Plastic food storage containers (tubs, boxes, and bowls) make ideal small water features—especially once you have covered the naked plastic. An easy decorating technique involves the use of "hypertufa," the home-made mixture that rock and alpine gardeners use to create tub and trough gardens. Combine equal parts of vermiculite, Quikrete brand concrete (available at most hardware stores), and long-grain (un-milled) sphagnum moss with enough water to create a thick batter. If you like, add a little concrete dye, available in many colors (wear disposable plastic gloves, as the dye stains the skin). Cover the outer surfaces with the mix, leaving the bottom for last, inverting the container, and, working quickly, covering the exposed bottom surface. Let it dry for several hours. Then turn the plastic ware right side up and cover any exposed lip surfaces with more freshly made mixture (hypertufa hardens very quickly). Let it dry for a couple of days. Try covering a ubiquitous plastic window box with hypertufa to create a remarkable window water feature. Plug up the drainage holes with silicone aquarium sealant.

SOIL CONSIDERATIONS AND POTTING

As they evolved in eutrophic (nutrient-rich) waters, most aquatic plants require soil that's very high in organic matter to grow luxuriantly. However, organic components often throw the aqueous ecosystem out of balance—especially in small containers—and produce an excess of methane gas, resulting in a depressing, malodorous mess. Potting soils for water plants, therefore, are typically clay or sand based and contain little or no organic matter. To provide the plants with the nutrients they require, it's best to use specially formulated fertilizer tablets.

To install your miniature water garden, set the individual plants in appropriately sized plastic or terra-cotta pots or fiberglass or wooden crates and place them in the watertight container.

SUMMER CARE

Summertime care of small water features—removal of dead foliage and spent blossoms, weeding, organic pest control and fertilization regimens—is exactly the same as for their in-ground counterparts. However, instead of donning rubber waders, slip on a rubber glove. And the size of the tools may change: Manicure scissors may replace standard shears, spoons and forks displace shovels and spades, and a tiny aquarium net supplants its full-sized equivalent.

OVERWINTERING AQUATIC PLANTS
IN COLD CLIMATES

Autumn is the time to begin listening to the weather report. When the first hard frost is on its way, you need to leap into action. Depending on the region that you live in, the critical moment may come any time between late August and late November. A hard freeze will destroy the foliage of hardy aquatics but not their

root systems, and will send perennial aquatic plants into "dormancy mode." That's when the overwintering procedures begin.

Empty all containers of water and store them inverted. Ceramic, porcelain, crockery, glass, and stoneware, as well as hypertufa-covered plastic should be stored in a frost-free environment—an unheated basement or attic, for example. Wooden bar-

Care for your water garden during the summer in the same way as you do any other plants.

35

rels are less cold-sensitive and can be stored empty in a garage or garden shed.

Although many people prefer to discard their plants at the end of the growing season (a financial luxury that not all of us possess), there are ways to overwinter desirable specimens. Remember that hardy herbaceous perennials require a true dormant period in order to remain healthy. Storing the plants in unheated indoor aquaria (with or without artificial illumination) is not an option, as the plants will eventually burn out because they can never rest. Their slow demise may take years.

Gardeners who have some space can plant the potted aquatics directly into the soil. An area that holds moisture well (a poorly drained spot at the bottom of a grade, for example) is best. Keep the interred plants potted to discourage them from rooting into the ground. Mulch the site after a long cold period—the idea is to keep the plants frozen, not snugly warm. The following spring, dig up the plants, then clean, divide, and repot them. An alternative is to place the potted plants in a plastic tub set inside a milk crate. Fill in the empty spaces above and between the pots with an insulating layer of dry straw and store the crate in an unheated garage or basement. Check your plants on a weekly basis and water if necessary throughout the winter months. They should be kept moist, but not soggy.

Make a trough water garden by covering an existing plastic container with homemade "hypertufa."

MINIATURE WATER-LILY

Nymphaea species and culti-vars—Not surprisingly, miniature water-lilies are by far the most coveted plants for medium, small, and miniature water gardens. They can be cultivated in containers as little as 12 to 18 inches wide and 4 to 10 inches deep, and are gener-ally hardy to Zone 4. Their tuberous creeping rootstock grows in a distinctly hori-zontal fashion, so plant them in a small azalea pot or a tiny plastic crate. White-flow-ered *Nymphaea tetragona*,

Miniature water-lilies, grown in a small pot.

yellow-blossoming *N. × helvola*, and bright red *N.* 'Perry's Baby Red' are only a tiny sampling of the available selection of magnificent minis.

MINIATURE LOTUS *Nelumbo nucifera*—Lotus require two to three sum-mer months of temperatures between 75 and 80° F. to initiate flowering. They have a robustly horizontal growth habit and should be planted in a flat plastic tub or crate submerged in a round decorative container. These particularly buoyant tuberous plants need to be weighted down with stones until the rootstocks have taken hold. Even the dwarf and semi-dwarf culti-vars are vigorous and require far more room than miniature water-lilies. Some choice small cultivars include: *Nelumbo* 'Baby Doll', which grows 24 to 30 inches tall and produces lovely, slightly fragrant, 4- to 6-inch white flowers, perfect for tub culture, and 'Chawan Basu', a 2- to 3-foot plant, which displays 5- to 9-inch ivory-white flowers with deep pink margins and venation. Another choice dwarf is 'Momo Batan'. It attains a height of 2 to 3 feet and produces 3- to 4-inch deep pink flowers, which are delightfully scented. But the jewel in the crown of minis belongs to the 1999 introduc-tion 'Little Tom Thumb'. Its pink, white, and green double flowers are 3 to 6 inches across, on a plant merely 8 inches tall. Dwarf and semi-dwarf lotus cultivars are reliably hardy to Zones 4 and 5.

YELLOW FLOATING HEART *Nymphoides peltata*—If your container is too small for even a miniature water-lily, then the yellow floating heart is perfect for you! It has floating, reddish mottled, heart-shaped foliage (reminiscent of *Nymphaea × helvola*) and, in spring, dainty, fringed yellow blossoms held 2 to 3 inches above the water's surface. It prefers a sunny position, but can be maintained in half-shade, although it will not reliably bloom. It is happiest in water at least 6 inches deep and is hardy to Zone 6.

WATER POPPY *Hydrocleys nymphoides*—This charming tropical plant has thick, shiny, deep green, broadly heart-shaped, 2- to 4-inch leaves. The pretty 2- to 2½-inch flowers are distinctly poppy-like, light yellow with red and brown centers. They are prolifically produced and held well above the foliage. Water poppies are tender and can be grown outdoors year-round only in tropical or subtropical areas. They can be overwintered in heated indoor aquaria or greenhouses. They prefer to grow in shallow water about 6 inches deep.

WATER CLOVER *Marsilea quadrifolia*—This intriguing, delicate plant is a true aquatic fern. A native of Europe and northern Asia, it has been introduced widely into the northeastern United States. Water clover is surprisingly hardy, surviving to Zone 5. It is perfect for the little shaded water garden, and the floating fronds, divided into two pairs of leaflets, are delicate and handsome. It can be successfully overwintered indoors in an unheated, illuminated aquarium.

Water poppy prefers shallow water.

ACORUS OR JAPANESE SWEET FLAG *Acorus gramineus*—This decorative aroid is cultivated for its handsome, architecturally linear, often variegated foliage, which generally doesn't exceed 9 inches tall. Although it its most often seen as indoor cold water aquarium plants, it is reliably hardy through Zone 5. It can be grown in sun or half-shade. The Japanese have introduced some truly remarkable variegated cultivars: 'Albovariegatus' (synonymous with 'Argenteostriatus') has white-striped 9-inch foliage. 'Variegatus' (syn. 'Aureovariegatus') has yellow-striped leaves. 'Oborozuki' has vibrant yellow foliage, and 'Ogon' (syn. 'Wogon') bears variegated chartreuse and cream leaves. 'Yodo-no-yuki' has leaves striped with pale green. The most spectacular by far is 'Hime Masamune', which has more white in the foliage than the others, giving the clumps a shiny, silvery appearance. The most diminutive of all, 'Pusillus', is variegated white, dwarf, and compact, about 2 inches tall.

MINIATURE CATTAILS *Typha minima*—These graceful plants add an attractive verticality to even the tiniest water garden and are hardy to Zone 6. Their dainty inflorescences, picked and dried before the pollen is released, are wonderful additions to tiny dried flower arrangements. Growing no more than 12 to 18 inches tall, miniature cattails prefer a sunny location but can be maintained in half-shade, although they may not flower. Anchor them with stones so they don't topple in high winds.

SOFT RUSH OR JAPANESE MAT RUSH *Juncus effusus*—This straight sedge-like plant, native to Eurasia, provides the raw material for the ubiquitous woven Japanese *tatami* mats. It is assuredly hardy to Zone 4. Although it prefers full sun, it is quite forgiving. The species grows to about 3 feet tall and is a little straggly for small water gardens. However, a couple of cultivars are quite worthy for small water features: 'Spiralis', a 15-inch plant (which doesn't grow quite as tall when cultured in a small pot), bears dark green, contorted, corkscrew-shaped needle-like foliage. It is an altogether striking marginal plant (growing in damp soil at the water's edge in the wild), as is 'Vittatus', with thick, quill-like foliage narrowly banded with ivory. It grows to about 30 inches or less in height.

Water clover is a true aquatic fern.

39

HARDY CACTI AND SUCCULENT GARDENS

ELLEN ZACHOS

TO MOST OF US, CACTI AND SUCCULENTS are classic desert plants. We think of the imposing Saguaro cactus in Arizona and can't imagine having something similar in our urban or suburban gardens. In fact, cacti and succulents tolerate a wide variety of growing conditions, and many are hardy to Zone 4. If you appreciate these architectural plants, you can easily feature a few containers of hardy specimens, no matter where you live. Just be sure to locate them in a bright spot with at least six hours of sun per day.

Even a small display of cacti and succulents can include a great variety of shapes and colors: Spiky rosettes of yellow and green foliage surrounding flower stalks that are two feet tall, miniature succulent leaves with brilliant red color, clusters of hens and chicks covered with spidery cobwebs (*Sempervivum arachnoideum*) —these are just a few of the

Opposite and above: Many succulents are very hardy and can easily be grown in pots, provided they get at least six hours of sun per day.

contrasting forms you can combine. The size of your container will determine how many different plants to include. While you may be tempted to choose a large assortment of species, your container will look better if you limit yourself to between four and six distinct plant types. The plants should harmonize rather than compete for attention.

CONTAINERS

If your container is going to overwinter outdoors, it should be made of a frost-proof material such as fiberglass, cement, wood, or hypertufa. Most terra-cotta pots will crack as the soil inside them freezes and thaws. Make your choice based on practicality and aesthetics. If you love to constantly move and tweak the arrangement of your containers, be sure to choose something made of a lightweight material. And always use containers with adequate drainage holes.

Opposite and above: Before you start planting the succulent garden, picture how the heights and textures of your plants will interweave. Then place the largest plant, add some soil, and set the other plants from the center outwards.

Next, consider the depth of your container. All cacti and succulents, no matter where they grow, require quick drainage and will rot in damp soil. With a whiskey barrel or planter box full of cold, wet soil you are asking for trouble, since the large volume of soil will hold too much moisture close to the plants' roots. Try this trick to improve drainage: Place a layer of landscape cloth inside the bottom of the container and pour in a layer of polystyrene peanuts. You can also use pebbles, but remember that they will add considerable weight to the pot and make it hard to move. (How deep the layer should be depends on the depth of the container; six inches is about right for a container 18 to 24 inches tall.) Then, add another layer of landscape cloth. The second layer of cloth prevents the polystyrene from working its way up to the top. Now you're ready to add soil.

POTTING MIXES

When choosing a potting mix, remember that a lightweight commercial mix will drain more quickly than pure topsoil. Look for something that contains no more than 50 percent loam, with the balance made up of bark, compost, or sand. It is not necessary to purchase a special "cactus" mix. If you prefer to blend your own, try equal parts sand, soil, and leaf mold (or bark or compost), or, half soil, one-quarter sand, and a quarter leaf mold (or bark or compost). Both recipes provide quick-draining mixes that enable drought-tolerant plants to thrive.

PLANTING

Now you're ready to plant. Sit back, close your eyes, and envision the "skyline" of your garden. Where do you want the focus to be? Do you want a single high point in the middle of your pot? Would you like trailing succulents to soften the rim of your container? Can you picture how the various heights and textures of your plants will interweave? Take some time to sketch the basic shapes you'd like to include, making room for any favorite plants you feel you must incorporate. Before you actually plant, position the specimens in groups, to get an idea of how they will look together.

If your container is shallow and does not require the extra drainage layer described above, cover the drainage holes with landscape cloth. Add a layer of soil to the bottom of the container and place the largest plant first, adding plants from the center outwards. Be very gentle when you firm the soil around the roots because bruised roots invite rot. Don't crowd the plants. Remember, this container is going to be around for a while and you want to give everything room to grow. If the container feels too empty, or if you'd simply like to add a few accents, try placing stones for aesthetic interest.

WATER AND FERTILIZER

Don't water the cacti and succulent container right away. Inevitably, some roots will have been damaged in the planting process, and they should be allowed to callus before being watered. Three to five days should be plenty, depending on the season. After the initial watering, the plants will require relatively little attention. How often you need to water depends on the size of the pot or box. Even in summer, you will need to water a whiskey barrel planting only every two to four weeks. A small cement container may require weekly watering. Test the top inch of soil with your finger, and if it feels dry, it's safe to water.

Succulents and cacti prefer infrequent, thorough waterings to more frequent, superficial showers. A deep drenching allows the entire root system to soak up and store moisture, encouraging root growth throughout the container, rather than merely in the top layer of soil, where roots are most vulnerable. As the temperatures drop in fall, the plants enter dormancy and you should water less frequently, stopping altogether when the growing season ends. The occasional winter rain will probably be enough to sustain the cacti and succulents throughout their dormant period. If you notice them starting to shrivel, water sparingly.

These are flowering plants, and should be fertilized accordingly. A good soil mix will contain enough nutrients for the first growing season, and later you can feed as you would any perennial container planting; specialized cactus fertilizer is not necessary. A balanced plant fertilizer containing equal amounts of nitrogen, phosphorus, and potassium (with an N-P-K formula of 10-10-10, for example) improves general growth, while a bloom booster (a formula with a higher phosphorus content—the middle number) encourages flowering.

OVERWINTERING

Many cacti and succulents are evergreen and they need time to harden off before frost. Stop feeding cacti and succulents six to eight weeks before the first frost date for your area, so they stop producing soft young growth, which is easily damaged by cold temperatures.

Remember that plants growing in the ground are insulated from freezing temperatures by the soil. Succulents grown in containers have much less soil surrounding their roots and are therefore more vulnerable to the colder temperatures of winter. When choosing plants for a hardy succulent garden, pick some that are hardy to a colder zone than the one you live in, to ensure that they overwinter successfully. Also, after the first frost, when you put your garden to bed for the winter, consider wrapping the pots in burlap to give them extra insulation.

Listed below are ten cactus and succulent species that are both widely available and hardy to at least Zone 7 in containers. The list is by no means exhaustive, and you should experiment with any hardy specimen that catches your eye.

MESCAL *Agave parryi*—Native to Arizona and New Mexico, this is one of the most cold-hardy agaves around. It grows to 2 feet tall and 30 inches wide. It grows slowly and flowers after many years with a spike that's 12 to 15 feet tall.

HEDGEHOG CACTUS *Echinocereus triglochidiatus*—Hedgehog cactus grows to 6 inches tall and spreads up to 10 inches wide. Its brilliant

Mescal is very cold-hardy.

Hedgehog cactus blooms in early summer.

Opuntia humifusa is a hardy type of prickly pear cactus, native to the eastern and midwestern states.

crimson flowers in early summer are richly saturated and vibrant.

PRICKLY PEAR CACTUS
Opuntia humifusa (*compressa*)—This is a hardy prickly pear whose large green pads look deceptively smooth but are, in fact, covered with many needle-like spines. Its flowers are yellow or yellow and orange.

HYLOTELEPHIUM SIEBOLDII—A prostrate plant with blue-gray foliage, this former *Sedum* is a lovely accent plant. Its stems will cascade over the pot rim, and in October plants are topped with abundant dusky pink flowers.

HYLOTELEPHIUM 'AUTUMN JOY'—This well-known plant, formerly known as a *Sedum*, grows to 2 feet tall. Its large (6 inches across), flat flower heads deepen to a rich reddish rust color in September, and the foliage is an attractive glaucous grayish green throughout the growing season.

RED CARPET SEDUM *Sedum spurium* 'Red Carpet' and dragon's blood sedum *S. spurium* 'Schorbuser Blut'—Both have prostrate growing habits and grow to only 2 inches tall. Their ground-hugging foliage is dark red and strikingly beautiful, and they have pink to red flowers in summer.

Banana yucca, *Yucca baccata*, derives its common name from its flowers, which resemble tiny bananas.

SPIDERWEB HENS AND CHICKS *Sempervivum arachnoideum*—This is a species with small rosettes (approximately 1 inch wide) that are covered with silvery hairs resembling a spider's web, hence the common name.

HENS AND CHICKS *Sempervivum tectorum*—The rosettes of this species are larger than those of *S. arachnoideum*. They can be 3 to 4 inches wide and in summer produce reddish pink flowers on stems 8 to 12 inches high. The species is highly variable, and plants may exhibit glaucous foliage and/or reddish purple variegation.

BANANA YUCCA *Yucca baccata*—This yucca has thick, curved blue-green leaves edged in red, and grows to 8 inches high. Its name comes from the flowers, which are shaped like very small bananas.

VARIEGATED YUCCA *Yucca filamentosa* 'Variegata'—Growing to 18 inches tall, this yucca has straight, sword-like leaves. It can be found with cream-colored leaf edges and green centers or green edges and cream-colored centers. Both have long, curly threads along the leaf margins.

ALPINE ADVENTURES

ABBIE ZABAR

PLANTS THAT LIVE IN POTS remind me of my cats. Willy and Milly like a cozy place to curl up in, but they also need room to stretch. For over 30 years I've been gardening in containers…of sorts. Frequently, I've pushed the envelope. As long as I can provide adequate holes for drainage, I'm ready to turn all kinds of stuff—often what nobody even wants anymore—into perfect planters.

High above New York City, in soil-filled cavities that were chipped and chiseled out of granite pavers, I'm cultivating a collection of crevice-loving alpine plants. Appropriately called "rock breakers," in their elevated habitat these prostrate alpine plants grow so unrelentingly that they actually break down the

Alpine plants are used to the harsh conditions of wind-swept mountainous regions.

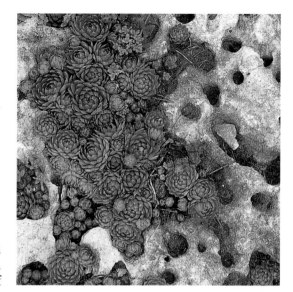

limestone rocks in which they root. For these plants, including representatives of the genera *Armeria* (sea pinks), *Dianthus* (pinks), *Draba*, and *Eriogonum* (wild buckwheat), all container-hardy from Zones 5 or 6 to 8, I create portable troughs from "lost and found" urban cobblestones. Like most gardeners, I was scavenging before recycling was the law. A well-stocked stoneyard will offer a more conventional (and legal) source for potential planters.

Alpine plants are usually diminutive survivors native to the nooks and crannies of mountainous regions. Their size and tightly formed leaves are adapted to extreme weather conditions: constant gale-

Top and bottom: *Sempervivum* doesn't need much soil, but like all alpines, it requires good drainage.

force winds, long bitter winters, and short growing seasons. Living at altitudes between the timberline and the ski line, they creep through cracks of rocks often no wider than a worm. I figured that a collection of hardy little alpines in appropriate containers might just acclimate in a garden that precipitously grows 21 stories above Central Park's tree line and outcroppings of glacially polished rock. Weather conditions up here can get nearly as dicey as on some mountain ranges—merciless sun and wind gusts so strong that air circulation is never a problem.

49

Adapted to extreme living conditions, alpine plants are well suited to a rooftop garden that is exposed to unrelenting sun and wind.

Just as Gertrude Jekyll devoted areas in her gardens to a particular plant or to those that would look showy in only one season, I cultivate a single variety of alpine in each cobblestone. I want it to be a compact grower with foliage that will form a tight little pillow. If I lean towards the lime-encrusted saxifrages, it's because the speckled silvery edges of their leaves make me notice the sparkling mica chips in their granite containers, and vice versa.

TINY POTS FOR MINIATURE PLANTS

What matters to me most is the scale of plant to pot. I'd like to think I make a big deal about proportion because I'm an artist and designer, not because I was one of the smallest kids in the class. I want my plants to be comfortable in their clothing. Even lifelong saxifrage (*Saxifraga paniculata* 'Minima'), which is hardy in pots from Zones 3 to 9, an itty-bitty bun of gray-green rosettes that will never be more than knuckle-high, should feel right about its garb. Another disarming saxifrage to consider is *S.* 'Cockscomb', with crested ridges down the middle of its leaves. It is pot-hardy from Zones 3 to 7.

You know those masonry blocks with slits where troweled cement goes? I covered the bottom holes of one with large clay shards, then planted a tuft of wooly thyme (*Thymus pseudolanuginosus*, hardy in pots to Zone 6) in it and, before long, the aromatic groundcover was sprawling all across the top like a floppy, thick toupee. It's one of many thymes among the herbs in small-scale pots on my rooftop garden. Other candidates to consider for diminutive domains include ground-hugging *Thymus* 'Reiter's Red' (1 inch, container-hardy from Zones 4 to 9) and *T. serpyllum* 'Minus', also called 'Minor', (½ inch, Zones 4 to 9), the smallest carpeter.

Over in the corner of the lower terrace I've got a trough with a "field" of slightly potbound—just the way they like it—farina-covered leaves of *Primula auricula* varieties. They prefer a moist, well-drained, limy soil and are container-hardy from Zones 5 to 8. "The first little thing of spring" is the charming translation of their botanical name. If I carry that 19th-century stone container, the size of a shoebox, inside where I'm writing, I'll be totally distracted by the sweet, yet sturdy, little miracle of springtime. Also in that corner of the terrace, there is a dark red, English clay flat—the kind Victorian nurserymen used for starting seedlings—seductively overflowing with enough hens and chicks of the *Sempervivum* 'King George' variety to be a scale model for the Hanging Gardens of Babylon. Other procumbent succulents to muse on include *Sempervivum* 'Silver Thaw' and the cobwebbed *S. arachnoideum* cultivars, container-hardy from Zones 6 to 8.

A GRITTY MIX

Alpine plants require excellent drainage, and when they're living in a variety of salvaged vessels, we gardeners can control the soil to keep them happy. I use a gritty mix of one part compost, one part potting soil, and one part coarse chick-

Each container is planted with a single variety of alpine plant. These are compact growers with foliage that is showcased by their tight little settings.

51

en grit (available at feed stores). Then I top-dress with crushed slag to keep the crown dry, because many alpines are susceptible to rot at that critical point. The rubble "mulch," which prevents the soil surface from baking in the sun, also inhibits weeds and adds a groomed appearance, admittedly with a Stone Age look.

But that's just the point. I'm paying homage to the thought that 15,000 years ago this steel and concrete city was a boulder-strewn landscape of just gravel, sand, and bare rocks. And today I garden at the top of an apartment building that sits on solid bedrock.

Lots of things I love growing look best—even flourish—in squat containers. Nothing illustrates this more than my up-in-the-air rock garden, where I'm able to keep an eye on a collection of favorite plants that, like a couple of cats, would certainly get lost in bigger gestures and grander spaces.

Spring-blooming *Primula auricula* makes a nice addition to an alpine trough garden.

UNUSUAL PLANTS FOR POTS

IN THIS SECTION YOU'LL find four chapters, each focusing on different types of plants that make ideal candidates for pots: hardy shrubs; drought-resistant perennials, annuals, vines, bulbs, shrubs, trees, groundcovers, and grasses; unusual herbs; and miniature vegetables.

HARDY SHRUBS FOR CONTAINERS

GARY R. KEIM

GARDENERS TEND TO THINK OF CONTAINER GARDENING as an activity for the spring and summer months. While it's true that the most dazzling displays of flower color occur at this time, it's definitely worthwhile to take a closer look at container gardening as a four-season endeavor. Container-hardy trees and shrubs make great candidates

for year-round display. When I seek a hardy plant for container growing, I want one that has multiple seasons of interest or an extremely long season of colorful foliage or interesting bark. Stems or fruit are a bonus and add another dimension to the potted garden.

First, let's define container hardiness. The rule of thumb used by experts: A plant is "container-hardy" only to two USDA hardiness zones warmer than its "in-ground" hardiness (see page 101 for a map of the USDA hardiness zones). To use an example, false cypress (*Chamaecyparis obtusa*), which is hardy to

Container-hardy trees and shrubs make great candidates for year-round display.

Evergreens like this false cypress give life to the bleak winter landscape, as do hardy shrubs with colorful berries or stems.

Zones 4 to 5 in the garden, will be container-hardy only to Zones 6 to 7. As with all rules, there are exceptions, and with trial and error you can find out what works in your location. Hardiness has much to do with container placement. Often, an area near a building has a relatively warm microclimate, especially if it has a sunny exposure. Sheltered from winter winds and bathed in sunlight, a particular location may be an entire hardiness zone warmer than the surrounding area. So, take advantage of a favorable spot near the house and place autumn- and winter-season containers where you can enjoy them from windows and as you pass to and from the home.

Some of my favorite container-hardy plants are perfectly hardy in the ground where I garden in Zone 6, but I choose to grow them in containers nonetheless, because I want them in a spot where I can enjoy them during the winter months. Others are hardy in the ground, but not container-hardy, so they require some winter protection. A few are not garden- or container-hardy in Zone 6, but would be perfectly container-hardy in other parts of the country. If I can get nine to ten months of enjoyment from a plant, I will be willing to go an extra step to keep it. My non-hardy pots move into a barely heated garage or unheated greenhouse during the coldest part of the winter. As the days begin to warm in March, I take them outdoors again.

To justify the maintenance of the pots throughout the year, I choose only hardy plants that hold my attention for a long period. If a plant can give me plea-

Come winter, Tartarian dogwood will reveal its deep red stems.

sure through the long winters of the Northeast, then I'm happy to include it in my container garden. Attractive berries, bark, and evergreen foliage are the key features that I look for. You can expect to keep most shrubs in container culture for three to five years, and then it is best to plant in the garden and start anew.

The selections that follow only hint at the possibilities that container gardening with hardy shrubs can offer. Be adventurous; explore further and discover additional choices.

SHRUBS WITH COLORFUL STEMS

YELLOW-TWIG DOGWOOD *Cornus sericea* 'Silver and Gold'—A supreme example of a four-season plant, this ornamental shrub (Zone 2) has green and cream variegated leaves during the growing season that drop in autumn to reveal bright yellow stems that catch the low winter sun. The stems can reach 6 to 8 feet (less in a pot), but it is best to cut them back to the base each spring because new stems will shine the brightest. Managed in this way, the stems will reach a height of 3 to 5 feet. I find the summer foliage most agreeable to combine with other potted plants. A close relative, Tartarian dogwood, *Cornus alba* 'Argenteomarginata' (Zone 3), has white and green variegated leaves and deep red winter stems.

CORAL-BARK WILLOW *Salix alba* 'Britzensis'—A shrubby willow good for containers, coral-bark willow (Zone 2) has narrow, linear leaves that clothe the shrub in summer, making it a fine textured backdrop for other container plants.

In the dim winter months, after it sheds its cloak of leaves and the stems glow a bright coral-red color, this plant lights up the landscape. Treat the stems in the same manner as the dogwood. Combine them with an evergreen background for a stunning statement.

HARRY LAUDER'S WALKING STICK *Corylus avellana* 'Contorta'—Another shrub grown for its winter branches, Harry Lauder's walking stick (Zone 4) admittedly is not one of the most attractive shrubs during the growing season. However, come winter, the twisted, corkscrew-like branches become a living sculpture. The sight of the branches covered with a fresh snowfall is a memorable image. Consider siting the pot in a less visible part of the garden during the summer and moving it to a prominent place in late autumn, preferably a spot with an evergreen backdrop to show the branches to best effect. The golden catkins that unfurl with the warming days of spring are a bonus.

During the growing season, yellow-twig dogwood has green and cream variegated leaves.

SHRUBS WITH COLORFUL BERRIES

WINTERBERRY *Ilex verticillata* 'Red Sprite'—Red fruit is the reason to grow this holly (Zone 3), as is its small stature, which makes it well suited to container growing. Medium-green leaves during the season obscure the fruit until it begins to ripen in autumn. This is another candidate for growing out of sight during the summer and moving into a prime location when it comes into its own.

VARIEGATED ROCKSPRAY COTONEASTER *Cotoneaster horizontalis* 'Variegatus'—While cotoneasters are a staple of commercial plantings, they need to be used with great care, as many species are invasive. Their overuse is probably due to the fact that they are tough plants that can endure abusive conditions. *Cotoneaster horizontalis* 'Variegatus' has tiny leaves ringed by a halo of cream

Move winterberry to a prominent place in fall when its berries begin to color.

variegation. The branching structure is akin to the bones of a fish radiating from its spine, making the plant quite beautiful even in winter in its leafless state.

BROAD-LEAFED EVERGREENS WITH COLORFUL FOLIAGE

Broad-leafed evergreens offer many opportunities to the savvy container gardener. Their deep green, tough, shiny leaves have a strong presence in the winter landscape. Keen plant propagators have selected many that sport variegation, often in gold or yellow, which makes for an eye-catching foliage display.

WINTER-CREEPER MOONSHADOW *Euonymus fortunei* Moonshadow™—The common winter-creeper euonymus, *Euonymus fortunei* (Zone 5), is invasive and should not be used in the garden, but there are many variegated cultivars that are worth growing in pots. The selection Moonshadow eclipses all the others. Broad leaves with bright yellow centers edged in dark green form low mounds one to two feet high, which are perfect for planting under larger shrubs. It is a four-season player in any container garden, since the foliage can combine with many spring bulbs and summer annuals and brighten dull winter days.

FALSE-HOLLY *Osmanthus heterophyllus* 'Goshiki'—This shrub (Zone 6) brings cream and light yellow streaked, spiny, holly-like leaves to the container garden. Dense in habit, plants can get large in time but take hand pruning well. It is the newest growth that is the brightest and most appealing. Visually strong enough to hold its own, the false-holly works as a specimen in a formal setting or as part of a cheerful holiday arrangement combined with winterberry holly.

TWO TENDER SHRUBS
TOO GOOD TO PASS UP

Many subtropical plants are suitable for container culture but do not have the constitution to remain outdoors for the entire winter season. We refer to them as "tender." Some plants are too good to pass up, as long as you can provide a space to overwinter them during the coldest weather (see page 96).

New Zealand flax, *Phormium tenax* (Zone 8), is one of my tender favorites. Tough, leathery, spiky leaves in a variety of colors arranged in large, upright fans make a statement in the potted landscape. This shrub can be striking playing it solo or can share the limelight with other tender plants in mixed tapestry containers. I overwinter mine in an unheated greenhouse, which is one zone warmer than the great outdoors and shelters the foliage from the desiccating winter winds. You can also keep it in an unheated room indoors. Many cultivars are available at nurseries or by mail order.

Coralberry, *Ardisia crenata* (Zone 8), is another one of my favorites. Glossy, wavy-edged, evergreen leaves on upright stems lend this shrub an air of distinction. In summer, tiny white flowers bloom in loose clusters, followed by green, rounded fruit. As the year progresses, the fruit slowly turns a rich red color, just in time for the holiday season—which is about the time I bring the plant indoors, where it makes an excellent houseplant. Amazingly, the fruit will stay on plants up to a year or more.

If you live north of Zone 8, move coralberry into the house for the coldest months. It makes an excellent temporary houseplant for the holiday season.

Korean boxwood is very hardy, ideal for pots.

HYBRID ELAEAGNUS *Elae-agnus × ebbingei* 'Gilt Edge'—Most striking at any time of the year are this shrub's 3- to 4-inch gold-ringed leaves. Grown mainly for its foliage impact, it can anchor any container grouping for twelve months of the year. Try combining it with blue pansies in spring, orange-red *Gomphrena* 'Strawberry Fields' in summer, bright yellow single mums in fall, and *Cornus sericea* 'Silver and Gold' in winter. Prune to maintain a pleasing shape.

BROAD-LEAFED EVERGREENS WITH GREEN FOLIAGE

JAPANESE HOLLY *Ilex crenata* 'Sky Pencil'—This is a columnar selection of Japanese holly (Zone 5). Use it as an exclamation point for container groupings, or let a pair flank a formal entrance to a house. The small, shiny green leaves catch the light, adding sheen to this architectural plant.

BOXWOOD *Buxus microphylla*—Similar in texture to Japanese holly, boxwood has countless cultivars. In mild parts of the country, many of these are suitable for container culture. Korean boxwood, *Buxus microphylla* var. *koreana* (Zone 4), is a hardier selection, making boxwood a candidate for container gardeners in colder areas. As with all boxwoods, shearing or plucking is necessary to shape it into topiaries or formal shapes. Ultimately, it reaches 3 to 4 feet, but it's best to keep it smaller for ease of handling.

EVERGREEN CONIFERS

Every winter grouping of containers should have at least one conifer. Once the deciduous woody plants shed their mantles of foliage and herbaceous plants die to the ground or stand erect with their dried stems, it is evergreens that give life to the bleak winter landscape.

FALSE CYPRESS *Chamaecyparis obtusa* 'Nana Gracilis'—One of the most handsome evergreen conifers, false cypress, hinoki in Japanese (Zone 5), has dark green scales loosely borne in fan-like sprays that give it a layered appearance.

The clean foliage and pyramidal growth habit to 6 feet lend an air of refinement to any part of the garden.

JUNIPER 'GREY OWL' *Juniperus virginiana* 'Grey Owl'—This horizontally growing shrub (warmer parts of Zone 3) has gray-green, spiky, needled foliage. Its unusual color contrasts well with green conifers, dark backgrounds, and many summer annuals. Junipers are drought-tolerant, perfect for gardeners who may be lax in their watering duties.

AMERICAN ARBORVITAE *Thuja occidentalis* 'Hetz Midget'— Relegated to the unfashionable list because of many years of overuse in mundane foundation plantings, 'Hetz Midget' (Zone 3) makes an ironclad container-grown conifer. It forms a rounded shape with soft scale-like needles, which are green in the warm months of the year and bronze during the winter season. Some people find this unattractive, but why must all evergreens be green? Capitalize on the somber color by combining it with a bright yellow-twig dogwood or a golden variegated euonymus.

MONTEREY CYPRESS *Cupressus macrocarpa* 'Golden Pillar'—With its soft chartreuse yellow needles, this Monterey cypress cultivar (Zone 8) is electric year-round. It's especially effective in spring with blue, orange, or purple pansies; in summer with orange marigolds, blue *Scaevola*, and black sweet potato vine; in fall with bronzy mums; and in winter with other evergreens. I prefer to shear my plant a couple of times a year to keep it tight and shapely. The growth habit is upright, and it can easily be trained to be a spire. A word of caution: Since this plant is hardy only to Zone 8, you will have to move it inside in winter. I usually enjoy it outdoors until the holiday season, then bring it in, where it thrives under normal indoor conditions.

Juniper 'Grey Owl' is drought-tolerant.

DROUGHT-RESISTANT PLANTS FOR POTS

ELLEN ZACHOS

IN RECENT YEARS, communities all over the United States have experienced some form of drought, and in response, many have restricted the use of water for gardening. As environmentally conscious gardeners, we need to find ways to create gardens—including container gardens—that require little, if any, supplemental watering.

In 1981, the Association of Landscapers and Contractors of Colorado coined the term "xeriscape." "Xeros" is Greek for dry and "scape" comes from the Anglo-Saxon "schap," meaning view. Xeriscape gardening promotes water conservation through inventive landscaping. It is water-efficient, but by no means restricted to stark collections of rocks and cacti. Drought-resistant container gardens need not sacrifice a variety of form and color. There's an additional benefit in planting a drought-tolerant potted garden—you will spend less time maintaining and more time enjoying it.

Fuzzy leaves are one sign that a plant is drought-tolerant.

Sunflowers make excellent accent plants and add height to the potted garden.

There are certain characteristics that indicate drought tolerance, so keep these in mind when choosing xerophytic plants for containers: Silvery foliage and hairy or fuzzy leaves reflect sunlight, thus reducing water loss via transpiration, the normal loss of water vapor from a plant's leaves. Leaf hairs also act as a physical barrier to transpiration by reducing air movement over the surface of the leaf. Succulent plant parts, like the leaves of rose moss (*Portulaca* species), store water for drier times. A thick cuticle (a waxy coating secreted by the plant's epidermal cells) slows the loss of water through the leaf surface. The leaves of ivy-leaved geranium, *Pelargonium peltatum,* have just such a cuticle. A taproot is another excellent water storage device. Plants with taproots, like butterfly weed (*Asclepias tuberosa*), store enough water to get through periods of drought.

DROUGHT-TOLERANT PLANTS

There are so many xerophytic plants that it would be impossible to include them all here. A good rule of thumb is to choose plants that are native to your area; a number of the non-native ornamentals recommended as drought-tolerant candidates for the garden have become invasive, threatening North American habitats and their associated plants and animals. Plants known to be invasive should not be used in regions where they have been noted as such or other regions with similar climates and growing conditions.

Plants grown in containers are more exposed to the elements than their peers growing in the ground, and therefore should be treated as less hardy. The hardiness listing provided for each perennial gives the zone to which that plant is reliably hardy in a container setting, which is generally two zones warmer than

Above: Butterflies love lantana, which is grown as an annual in cooler regions. Individual flowers change their color to yellow once they have been pollinated. Opposite: As the name suggests, North American native butterfly weed is another pollinator favorite. A long taproot makes this perennial very drought-resistant.

its USDA listing. For example, sea holly (*Eryngium bourgatii*) is hardy to Zone 5 when it grows in the ground and container-hardy to Zone 7. Please refer to page 101 for a map of the USDA hardiness zones.

HERBACEOUS PERENNIALS

SEA HOLLY *Eryngium bourgatii*—This plant has a wonderful structure and is exceedingly tough. Its leaves are stiff and marked by white veins that complement the spiny, silvery white flower bracts. It is container-hardy to Zone 7 and grows to 24 inches tall.

PERENNIAL FLAX *Linum perenne*—The flowers of perennial flax are a deep, clear, true blue. They open in the heat of day and close again by evening. This easy-to-grow plant does best in full sun and well-drained soil. It's container-hardy to Zone 7 and reaches 1 to 2 feet in height.

CONEFLOWER *Echinacea purpurea*—This drought-tolerant North American native grows best in sandy soil and full sun. The white cultivars are especially attractive and grow to 24 inches tall. This makes them somewhat shorter than their more common pink cousin. All *Echinacea* bloom from July through August and are container-hardy to Zone 6.

GLOBE THISTLE *Echinops bannaticus*—This thistle has long-lasting, pale blue, globe-shaped flowers that make excellent cut and dried displays. Foliage and growth habit are also very attractive. Globe thistle is container-hardy to Zone 6 and reaches 2 to 3 feet tall (depending on the cultivar).

BUTTERFLY WEED *Asclepias tuberosa*—Its taproot makes this North American native an especially drought-tolerant choice, and its flowers attract bees and butterflies to your garden in abundance. Cultivars range from 1 to 3 feet in height, with flowers available in yellow, orange, vermilion, or white. It is container-hardy to Zone 6.

ANNUALS

LANTANA *Lantana* species—Available in numerous colors, including yellow, orange, red, white, pink, and lavender, lantana—or shrub verbena, as it is often called—comes in both upright (*Lantana camara*) and weeping forms (*Lantana montevidensis*). The leaves have a spicy fragrance, and the plant will flower all summer long if conscientiously dead-headed. Seed heads are also attractive and mature to a shiny, blue-black fruit. (In frost-free areas, *Lantana camara* is hardy and will grow into a shrub.)

SUNFLOWER *Helianthus annuus*—The many varieties range from 2 to 12 feet tall and offer flowers in white, yellow, orange, or red. Some cultivars have huge, single flowerheads, while others have several flowers per stalk. All make excellent accent plants and add height to your containers.

BLUE MARGUERITE *Felicia amelloides*—This marguerite has lovely blue petals surrounding a yellow center. It ranges from 1 to 3 feet tall and grows best in full sun. This annual flowers best in cool weather, so use it for early spring bloom, then cut it back for another round of flowers in fall.

ZINNIA *Zinnia angustifolia*—Available with white or orange flowers, both with yellow-orange centers, Mexican zinnia grows 8 to 12 inches tall and is quite drought-tolerant. The plant flowers profusely, and its leaves are an attractive gray-green with a linear shape. It is sometimes sold as *Zinnia linearis*.

IVY-LEAVED GERANIUM *Pelargonium peltatum*—Dark green, shiny leaves and a trailing growth habit make this plant particularly valuable for container culture. Its blooms are not as large as those on some other geraniums but the color and shape are lovely, and its foliage helps weave together the diverse contents of your container.

ANNUAL AND PERENNIAL VINES

BOUGAINVILLEA—Nothing beats the brilliance of *Bougainvillea*. An annual in the North, it's a fast grower, with solid green- or white-variegated leaves and colorful petal-like bracts (not flowers) that can be magenta, white, yellow, orange, or pink. Cut it back and bring it indoors for the winter if you have a sunny window.

Tender *Bougainvillea* (left) and hardy trumpet creeper (right), favorite vines for pots.

TRUMPET CREEPER *Campsis radicans*—An excellent choice to cover a trellis or arbor, this North American native vine grows quickly and gives good coverage within two or three years. Flowers can be shades of orange or yellow, depending on the cultivar, and the vine blooms for several months in summer. It is container-hardy to Zone 7.

MORNING GLORY *Ipomoea tricolor*—The classic "morning glory blue" is a true symbol of summer, but a rich array of purples, pinks, and stripes are also worth growing. *Ipomoea* grows quickly and prefers sandy, poor soil. It can easily cover a full-sized tree or two-story house in a single growing season.

SWEET AUTUMN CLEMATIS *Clematis terniflora*—This vine delivers a blast of bloom just when you need it: in autumn, when thoughts of winter creep into every gardener's brain, Throughout the summer, its attractive, three-lobed leaves nicely cover an arbor or fence. In early fall, the profusion of white blooms is the finishing touch. The vine, often sold as *Clematis paniculata,* is container-hardy to Zone 7.

CAPE LEADWORT *Plumbago auriculata*—The flowers of cape leadwort are usually a clear pale blue, although a white cultivar is also available. Dead-heading helps guarantee bloom throughout the summer season. This vine is tender north of Zone 9, but just like *Bougainvillea,* it can be cut back in fall and over-wintered indoors.

BULBS

SNOWDROP *Galanthus nivalis*—It is impossible to overpraise this earliest harbinger of spring. Snowdrop makes a fragrant cut flower, although its scent isn't discernible in the cold winter air. On a warm day, or indoors, its perfume is lovely and delicate. Snowdrops bloom in late winter, and the foliage disappears when the plant goes dormant in mid-spring.

BEARDED IRIS *Iris germanica* —The many bearded iris hybrids offer a huge range of color choices, including purples, whites, golds, pinks, and reds. Flowers are intricate and showy, and the upright foliage is an excellent accent for the container garden, even when the plant is not in bloom.

Tulipa tarda is a reliable perennial bulb.

TULIPA TARDA—While some tulips can be temperamental, *Tulipa tarda* is an outstanding, reliable, hardy, drought-tolerant perennial. It blooms in April, and its brilliant, two-toned flowers are real showstoppers.

ONION *Allium* species—There are many alliums to choose from, all of them quite drought-tolerant. Heights range from 6 inches to 3 feet, and umbels come in many shades of purple and blue as well as yellow and pink.

FALL-BLOOMING CROCUS *Crocus speciosus*—This crocus blooms without foliage. Its flowers are considerably larger than those of the spring-blooming crocus, and it grows well in sandy, well-drained soils. Full sun is best, but some shade is fine.

SHRUBS

BLUEMIST SPIREA *Caryopteris × clandonensis*— This is an outstanding shrub with blue flowers in August and September. It blooms best in full sun and a well-drained soil, and is container-hardy to Zone 7. Its attractive gray-green foliage has a spicy scent. Treat this shrub, also called bluebeard and false blue spirea, as a perennial and cut it back to the ground in late winter; flowers are borne on new growth.

CRANBERRY COTONEASTER *Cotoneaster apiculatus*—This low-growing shrub has an attractive, stiff branching pattern. Its small leaves are shiny and the plant is covered with cranberry-red fruit. It is container-hardy to Zone 7 and its cascading growth habit is especially useful at the front of a large container.

Cranberry cotoneaster.

OREGON GRAPE *Mahonia aquifolium*—A lovely shrub with blue-green, spiky leaflets, it is container-hardy to Zone 7 and can take some shade. Yellow flowers are borne in spring, followed by grape-shaped (non-edible) fruit. This evergreen shrub grows to approximately 3 feet tall.

JAPANESE HOLLY *Ilex crenata*—A small-leafed evergreen with black berries borne on female plants, this holly is more drought-tolerant than most and grows best in well-drained soils. It grows well in sun or shade and is container-hardy to Zone 7.

SPIREA *Spiraea thunbergii*—One of the earliest spring-flowering shrubs, it has numerous white flowers. The

Evergreen Oregon grape flowers yellow and has blue-black fruit in fall.

foliage of this bushy plant turns a pretty orange-yellow in fall. Prune it to keep it in shape. It is container-hardy to Zone 6.

SMALL TREES

PURPLELEAF SAND CHERRY *Prunus* × *cistena*—The purple foliage makes this tree an excellent and valuable accent plant. Grow it as a multi-stemmed shrub or a small tree. It is container-hardy to Zone 4.

APRICOT *Prunus armeniaca*—This attractive small tree has pretty pink flowers in April or May, followed by edible fruit in July and August. This apricot is container-hardy to Zone 6.

COLORADO BRISTLECONE PINE *Pinus aristata*—The needles of this slow-growing North American native evergreen have an attractive bluish cast. Its picturesque growth habit is reminiscent of a trained bonsai and makes this plant a natural focal point. It is container-hardy to Zone 6.

DOWNY SERVICEBERRY *Amelanchier arborea*—This North American native has several things to recommend it. Delicate, white flowers precede foliage in very early spring and its gray bark is lovely year-round. This *Amelanchier* is the most drought-tolerant of the genus, grows in sun or shade, and is container-hardy to Zone 6.

Ground-hugging carpet bugleweed spreads quickly by stolons.

BLACK-HAW *Viburnum prunifolium*—An incredibly tough North American native, black-haw or plum-leaf viburnum, as it is also known, tolerates dry conditions and will grow in partial shade or sun. White, flat-topped flowers in May are followed by black fruit in September. This tree has reddish purple fall color and is container-hardy to Zone 5.

GROUNDCOVERS

CARPET BUGLEWEED *Ajuga reptans*—This is an attractive groundcover all summer long that comes in a wide variety of foliage colors (bronze, purple, white, green). Lovely purple-blue flowers cover the plant in spring. It grows quickly, spreading by stolons, and is container-hardy to Zone 5.

COMMON BEARBERRY *Arctostaphylos uva-ursi*—This North American native is a slow grower but worth waiting for. It's container-hardy to Zone 5, and its evergreen foliage takes on a pretty bronze tint in winter. Long-lasting red berries follow pink, bell-shaped spring flowers.

CREEPING JUNIPER *Juniperus horizontalis*—A tough North American native whose prostrate growth habit is well suited to draping a container edge. Container-hardy to Zone 5, its numerous cultivars offer varying shades of evergreen foliage, including blue-green, gray-blue, and dark green. Blue berries are an added bonus.

Left: Bearberry, a native groundcover. Right: Fountain grass, with fuzzy flower spikes.

CLIFF GREEN *Paxistima canbyi*—A North American native evergreen shrub with a low growth habit that makes it a useful groundcover. It's container-hardy to Zone 6 and will grow in sun or shade. Well-drained sandy soil is best. Leaves are small and linear and turn bronze in fall.

WOOLY THYME *Thymus pseudolanuginosus*—The creeping growth habit of this thyme is particularly useful in containers, allowing it to fill in the gaps between neighboring plants. Its leaves are fuzzy, fragrant, and very tough. This herb is container-hardy to Zone 6.

ORNAMENTAL GRASSES

FEATHER REED GRASS *Calamagrostis* × *acutiflora* 'Karl Foerster' (syn. 'Stricta')—The botanical name is a mouthful, but worth learning to pronounce. This grass has a narrow, upright growth habit, reaches 5 feet in height, and needs full sun. It blooms in summer and its panicles are persistent, adding winter interest to your container. It is container-hardy to Zone 7.

BIG BLUE STEM *Andropogon gerardii*—This native North American grass once covered the prairies. It grows to 4 to 6 feet tall in containers, and its silvery blue foliage is truly beautiful. In fall, stems turn a striking coppery color. This grass grows best in full sun and is container-hardy to Zone 6.

MAIDEN GRASS *Miscanthus sinensis* 'Gracillimus' and zebra grass (*M. sinensis* 'Zebrinus') are two cultivars of *Miscanthus* with a clumping habit and a moderate growth rate. 'Gracillimus' reaches 5 to 6 feet tall and is topped by showy flowers in October. 'Zebrinus' has horizontal yellow stripes and reaches 7 feet tall. Both are hardy to Zone 7 and provide excellent winter interest. Maiden grass is invasive in some areas throughout the eastern U.S., from Florida to Texas, north to Massachusetts and New York. People who live in areas where maiden grass has proven problematic should refrain from growing it.

XERISCAPING TIPS
FOR CONTAINER GARDENERS

Container gardening presents its own set of challenges, among them more stressful growing conditions: As it holds only a limited amount of soil, a container offers limited room for roots to spread, dries out faster, and has a higher soil temperature. The following tips are based on principles formulated by the National Xeriscape Council, Inc., a non-profit organization, which serves as an informational clearinghouse for people interested in xeriscaping (see "For More Information," page 105).

PLAN AHEAD: Consider where you're placing your containers. For example, a spot in the sun can be 20° F. hotter than a nearby spot in the shade, so put your most drought-tolerant plants in the most exposed part of the garden. Trellises and arbors, as well as trees, create useful pockets of shade, so take advantage of them. In addition, group only plants with similar water requirements in the same container. By choosing plants with similar requirements, you can reduce water waste and improve your plants' health, since each will receive what it needs; no more, no less. If you want to include a few water-lovers in your garden, select shade-tolerant varieties, and place the container in the shade.

SELECT APPROPRIATE PLANTS: Choose plants suited to your region and microclimate. You've got some leeway here, because xeriscaping can mean different things in different parts of the country, depending on average temperature and rainfall. Start by looking at plants native to the drier habitats in your area; these plants frequently thrive without supplemental water.

IMPROVE THE POTTING MIX: Use a potting mix that's quick-draining, water-retentive, and nutrient-rich. Consider adding an inorganic soil conditioner to your mix. Water-retaining polymers (hydrogels), for example, hold several hundred times their weight in water and release it gradually to the plants' roots; one teaspoon absorbs one quart of water. Finally, mycorrhizal fungi improve the ability of a plant to take up water and nutrients by work-

TUFTED FESCUE *Festuca amethystina*—A superb accent plant with beautiful gray-blue foliage topped by tan panicles of flowers in late summer. One of our smaller ornamental grasses, it grows to approximately 12 inches and does very well in containers. It is container-hardy to Zone 6, frequently evergreen, and can be cut back to the ground in early spring.

FOUNTAIN GRASS *Pennisetum setaceum*—An annual grass in the north and well worth growing for its long-lasting, beautiful, fuzzy flower spikes. Cultivars with coppery red spikes and foliage are particularly useful as accent plants. This grass grows to 24 to 36 inches tall, depending on the cultivar.

---

ing with the plant's root system. Packets of mycorrhizal fungi (combined with hydrogels, soil conditioners, and bio-stimulants) are available commercially and should be added to the soil before planting.

IRRIGATE EFFICIENTLY: If you use an irrigation system, minimize water waste by applying the water exactly where it is needed. If possible, use drip emitters to deliver water to each container in your potted garden; drip irrigation systems use about 30 to 50 percent less water than sprinkler systems. They are highly efficient, delivering water directly to the roots of the plants, minimizing evaporation and run-off.

USE MULCH: A two- to three-inch layer of mulch covering the soil surface will cool the soil and help it retain moisture. In fact, soil that's one inch below a layer of mulch can be up to 10° F. cooler than unmulched soil at the same depth. Mulch reduces weed growth and organic mulch improves the fertility of the soil as it decomposes. It also prevents crusting of the soil surface, allowing water to penetrate to the root zone. Finally, the dark color and uneven surface of mulch limits reflectivity. Sand and clay soils can be highly reflective and bounce heat and light up onto plants. The fragmented surface of mulch reduces reflectivity and cools the adjacent area. Shredded or chipped bark, compost, and cocoa hulls make excellent mulches and will help you conserve water.

MAINTAIN THE XERISCAPE: The initial soil preparation should be adequate for at least the first growing season. Do not overfertilize your xeriscape container garden, since this promotes weak growth that requires extra water. Keep pruning to a minimum as it actually encourages growth. Rather than pruning, research the growth habits of the plants you're interested in and pick only those that are the right size for your space. Be a vigilant weeder. Weeds compete with your plants for water and nutrients, thus increasing the total amount of water the container requires.

UNUSUAL HERBS FOR CONTAINERS

SCOTT D. APPELL

WHEN IT COMES TO GROWING HERBS in containers, many people don't experiment beyond garden center basics like sweet basil, oregano, thyme, and lavender. Whether you are cultivating herbs for their culinary importance or medicinal attributes, or simply because they smell great and look intriguing, it's worth trying unusual or little-known varieties.

Herbs can be divided into three basic horticultural groups: annual, perennial, and biennial. However, I think it makes more sense for container gardeners to separate them into two groups, depending on how wet they like their soil—those that prefer moist soils and those that relish drier conditions. When planning a potted herb garden, be sure to keep the two different cultural types separate. In a mixed planting that is kept moist, drought-loving herbs like oregano, sage, rosemary, thyme, and lavender will rot. Conversely, in a mixed planting that is kept on the dry side, moisture-lovers like mint, parsley, chives, and basil will wither. To guarantee success, plant herbs with similar watering needs together.

Whether moisture-loving or drought-tolerant, many herbs prefer fertile soil that drains well: Overwatering is the number one cause of death for container-grown herbs. Purchase good-quality packaged soil. Nowadays, like food items, packaged soils must list ingredients on the label. Look for organic ingredients like compost, decomposed manure, horticultural charcoal, and ground oyster shells. Mix in one-quarter (by volume) coarse sand to improve drainage. Moisture-lovers, such as parsley, basil, chives, mint, lemon grass, and stevia, prefer to keep their feet a little damp at all times. So, do not mix sand in the potting mix for these herbs; instead, incorporate more compost or peat moss to improve the soil's capacity to retain water.

Opposite: When planting a potted herb garden, be sure to keep drought-tolerant herbs like rosemary separate from moisture-lovers like basil and lemon grass.

The leaves of stevia taste very sweet.

For container plantings that remain undisturbed for a long time, such as large strawberry jars or half whiskey barrels planted with perennial herbs, add soil amendments like New Jersey greensand, cottonseed meal, and bone meal to round out the mixture. Follow the package directions.

Unless you garden in an area that is mild and frost-free, winterization techniques are an integral part of growing herbs in containers. Use durable, crack-resistant containers, such as the new fiberglass terra-cotta look-alikes or wood. Raise urns, tubs, or planter boxes filled with perennial herbs on pot feet to allow for better drainage—perpetually soggy roots are a serious problem—and move the containers next to a west-, south-, or east-facing wall or fence, which will act as a windbreak and provide a modicum of heat retention. Discard or compost annual herbs at the end of the growing season and store the empty containers in a frost-free garage or work shed.

Following are some unusual herb varieties suitable for containers.

EAST INDIAN OR TREE BASIL *Ocimum gratissimum*—Although basil can hardly be called unusual, this rare and highly desirable species is worth locating. A native of West and tropical Africa, it has pungently clove-scented foliage up to 6 inches long. Depending on your palate, the foliage can stand in for sweet basil (*O. basilicum*) in any of your favorite recipes. Amazingly, this basil attains 6 feet in height and develops thick woody stems, which lend themselves to culinary techniques that are not suitable for the more familiar sweet basil. Try using the freshly cut shrubby stems as flavor-imparting skewers for vegetable brochettes. Use them as trussing needles for poultry and fish, and when you're grilling, throw the stems onto the charcoal to impart a smoky basil flavor to grilled pizza or foccacia. This plant, like other basils, prefers full sun and evenly moist soil. Seedlings are particularly sensitive to overwatering. Tree basil is hardy to Zone 10.

SWEET-HERB OF PARAGUAY OR SUGAR LEAF *Stevia rebaudiana*—Although stevia was once uncommon in cultivation, it has become increasingly available. The leaves contain stevioside, a substance that's 300 times sweeter than sucrose. These Brazilian and Paraguayan species grow to several feet tall on woody stems similar to those of their composite cousins, the asters and chrysanthemums. The foliage is slightly pubescent (fuzzy), with dentate (toothed) or crenulate (wavy-edged) margins. Dry the leaves and grind them as a sweetener or soak them in water and use the resulting liquid for teas, preserves, or juices. Try using the shrubby stems as skewers for grilled fruit brochettes or meat kebabs, and sprinkle the foliage as a sweetly edible garnish on fruit salads and baked goods. *Stevia*, which is hardy to Zone 9, prefers an evenly moist soil and can be overwintered indoors in northern climes.

Rosemary, lavender, thyme, salvia, and sweet pea make a handsome potted garden.

PERILLA OR BEEFSTEAK PLANT *Perilla frutescens*—Aficionados of Japanese cuisine know this plant as shiso, the ubiquitous aromatic fresh or pickled accompaniment to plates of *sushi* and *sashimi*. The foliage of this annual herb, which has a distinctly coleus-like appearance, makes an excellent addition to raw salads or an edible garnish for all types of Asian cuisine. Perilla prefers a sunny exposure and a rich, evenly moist (but not soggy) soil and reseeds eagerly, so much so that it's been classified as a noxious weed in the mid-Atlantic. It is native from India to Japan and an important plant in Chinese herbal medicine. Some worthwhile cultivars include 'Aka Shiso' (also called 'Purple Crispy'), featuring reddish purple leaves with a cinnamon-like aroma. 'Green Cumin' is a rare type of perilla with cumin-scented foliage. A large-leafed, mild-flavored Korean selection is 'Kkaennip', with foliage 6 inches in diameter. It is often used as a vegetable in stir-fries and for pickling. Perilla is hardy to Zone 8 and quickly grows to 2 to 3 feet in height.

CUBAN OREGANO *Plectranthus amboinicus*—Once a common Victorian annual bedding and conservatory plant, *Plectranthus amboinicus,* also known as Spanish thyme and Mexican mint, disappeared into obscurity but has recently enjoyed a horticultural renaissance. The common names are quite misleading— the herb is a native of Africa and undoubtedly came to the New World via the slave trade. The thick hairy leaves have a distinctly oregano-like aroma and flavor, and the plant resembles a furry, creeping coleus, to which it is related. Hardy to Zone 10, it relishes a fertile, well-drained soil and full sun, and is remarkably drought-resistant. The decumbent (trailing) growth habit makes

Homegrown lemon grass tastes delicious.

the plant suitable for hanging baskets and window boxes. In parts of Africa, Cuban oregano is used to flavor goat or fish dishes or as a potherb. In India, the leaves are used to flavor beer and wine. The Vietnamese use the leaves to flavor their famed sour soup. The foliage is a little thick and too furry to be enjoyed raw in salads, but it makes an excellent addition to cooked dishes from frittatas to chiles, ragouts, and tomato sauces. Cuban oregano is easy to overwinter on a sunny windowsill. The cultivar 'Variegata' has handsome, white-margined foliage.

CARDAMOM *Elettaria cardamomum*— The deliciously aromatic seeds of this tropical ginger relative are ground and used as a flavoring in some Dutch and Danish pastry recipes as well as in curry powder blends, cordials, gingerbread, bitters, sausages, and pickles. In India and other Asian countries, the seeds are chewed after meals to sweeten the breath. Cardamom, an Indian native that's hardy to Zone 10, rarely blooms and sets seed in northern latitudes. However, you can eat the young shoots raw, steamed, or roasted. Add a whole leaf or two to basmati rice prior to cooking to impart a wonderful fragrance and taste. In China, cardamom seeds are used medicinally to stimulate gastric activity and increase menstrual flow, and to treat premature ejaculation, incontinence, and stomachache. Like its cousin ginger, *Elettaria* has a creeping rhizome that produces shoots with two rows of broad, dark green fragrant leaves. It prefers a semi-shady spot and soil that is rich and water-retentive. Overwinter it indoors on a windowsill or in a greenhouse.

ROSEMARY *Rosmarinus officinalis* 'Arp' —Rosemary is another herb that needs no introduction, but a superior cultivar is certainly worth acquiring. Try the selection 'Arp', named after the city in Texas where, in 1972, it was found growing by Madalene Hill (co-author of *Gourmet Herbs: Classic and Unusual Herbs for Your Garden and Your Table*, Brooklyn Botanic Garden, 2001). It is the hardiest cultivar to date—to Zone 6, making it container garden-worthy, indeed. The needle-like foliage is light green and lemon-scented, and the flowers are light blue. It has an overall open growth habit and can attain a height of 5 feet under ideal conditions. The straight species is native to Southern Europe and North Africa. Rosemary prefers a very sunny position in fertile but flawlessly drained soil. Make sure you add plenty of coarse, sharp sand and horticultural charcoal to the potting mixture. Winter's soggy soils are the real menace of rosemary; place the container on pot feet to avoid excess moisture. In fall, move the container to a south-facing brick or stone wall, if possible, to aid as a heat-retentive wind break. Utilize 'Arp' as you would any other rosemary cultivar. Remember the woody twigs can be used as skewers for lamb or chicken kebabs, or thrown on the charcoal grill to impart their aromatic smell to other grilled foods. They make a soothing, incense-like addition to kindling for indoor fires, as well.

LEMON GRASS *Cymbopogon citratus*—Many people don't bother to grow this tropical lemon-scented grass; they prefer to purchase it from the greengrocer, where it is usually pre-wrapped and a little on the dry side. Homegrown plants are more aromatic and succulent, and their uprightly linear, grassy foliage perks up an otherwise leafy collection of potted herbs. The basal portions of the shoots are chopped and used to flavor fish, soups, sauces, teas, yogurts, and curries, but as the chopped foliage is a little tough to chew, it is always removed prior to serving the dish. Lemongrass is used in Greece and eastward throughout Asia. In China, the plant is boiled in water, which is then used to cure various ailments, including coughs and colds. Lemongrass is native to India and Sri Lanka and is hardy outdoors to Zone 9. It can attain a height of 5 to 6 feet and produces graceful, nodding flower panicles in summer. The herb appreciates a rich, moisture-retentive soil mixture and a sunny position. In addition to its culinary and medicinal attributes, lemongrass will impart a lovely lemony fragrance to steaming bath water and give fish or fowl a hint of delicate lemon flavor when strewn over the grill fire.

LION'S EAR *Leonotis leonurus*—This small shrub from eastern and southern Africa makes an unusual and beautiful addition to a sunny, drought-tolerant mixed container planting. It is a perfect butterfly and hummingbird plant. Wonderful whorls of orange tube-like flowers, which are produced late in the season like annual salvias, are impressive to behold and make terrific cut flowers. A series of potted specimens will make a profusely blooming division between garden rooms or flower beds or a beautiful seasonal container-grown hedge. The choice cultivar 'Harrismith White' has white blossoms. A woody annual that can withstand light frost with no ill effects, lion's ear is hardy to Zone 9, where it can become quite shrub-like and grow to 4 feet.

Lion's ear, a small African shrub.

MINIATURE VEGETABLES FOR CONTAINER GARDENS

SCOTT D. APPELL

I T IS NOT SURPRISING THAT MANY GARDENERS make good cooks. They bring the same attention to detail needed to cultivate vast varieties of edible plants, rare and common, into the kitchen when preparing a flaky broccoli quiche, baking a buoyant zucchini soufflé, or creating tiny hors d'oeuvres. It is all part of the same cycle: Propagate, cultivate, and transform the produce into fare for family and friends.

Many will remember the "baby vegetable" fad of the 1980s and early '90s, when every trendy upscale eatery nationwide offered diverse dishes of "baby" produce—literally immature (but edible) standard-sized peppers, eggplants, carrots, and zucchini, among others. In the meantime, professional vegetable growers and plant propagators have developed new vegetable cultivars that are truly diminutive, even when completely mature. Best of all, the new introductions produce their tiny crops on smaller plants, making them perfect candidates for little containers cultivated on modest patios, decks, terraces, or window ledges.

In order to harvest a tasty crop of container-grown produce, you need to place vegetable containers in a spot that gets six to eight hours of full sun a day. Select pots that are 12 to 16 inches in diameter or larger whenever possible, choosing the containers for width, not depth. Squat azalea-style pots, bulb pans, or concrete strawberry jars provide room for spreading root systems and a relatively low center of gravity, which will help keep containers from toppling over during summer storms.

Most vegetables require plenty of moisture. If you cultivate them in porous

Opposite: Recently introduced miniature vegetable cultivars produce tasty crops on small-scale plants, like the carrot 'Thumbelina'.

'Basket King' tomatoes grow nicely in a hanging basket.

terra-cotta or wood containers, they will need water more frequently than if you grow them in non-absorbent materials such as plastic or fiberglass. Use a soil mixture that's very rich and moisture-retentive, but well drained; many weekend container gardeners find the new, water-retaining polymer granules (hydrogels) a real boon. Never let your potted vegetables sit in a saucer of excess run-off water, and wherever possible, keep the pots elevated on pot feet to deter worms from entering through the drainage hole. Worms are beneficial in the garden soil, but detrimental to container-confined root systems. Amend the potting medium with compost, decomposed manure, ground oyster shell, pulverized eggshells (containerized tomatoes, in particular, are subject to calcium and boron deficiencies), greensand, horticultural charcoal, and coarse, sharp sand. Fertilize regularly with manure, compost "tea" (for a recipe, see "Soil Mixes, Potting Strategies, and Other Considerations," page 93), or fish emulsion, using them as foliar sprays, too. Never apply a fertilizer solution to dry soil: It may result in irreparable root burn and plant death. If the soil is dry, use plain water first, then follow up with the nutritive solution. In addition, do not use foliar chemical fertilizer sprays on hot, dry, sunny days: It may result in leaf burn. You can grow vegetables in slightly acidic or alkaline soils; they tolerate a pH range from 5.5 to 7.5 with no ill effects. Watch for insect pests, especially spider mites, where summers are hot and dry. Use your favorite organic pest controls and predatory insects to minimize any problems that may occur (see "For More Information," page 105).

Following are some of the miniature vegetable varieties suitable for container growing.

TOMATOES—Because growing tomatoes traditionally has been space-intensive, many hopeful container gardeners have been left empty-handed. However, recent introductions, such as 'Tiny Tim', which was developed specifically for pot culture, have redefined container gardening. Its dwarf habit makes it terrific for any container—even a hanging basket. It's loaded with 1- to 1¼-inch red cherry-style fruit that ripen very early. As an alternative, try 'Small Fry'.

PEPPERS—Pepper plants typically are just as large and shrubby as tomatoes, but miniature bell pepper 'Little Dipper Hybrid' produces just 2-inch-long fruit

Grow an abundant crop of hot peppers (left) and sweet bell peppers (right) in pots.

on 26-inch-tall plants. Early maturing and prolific, it produces green peppers that turn red. Dwarf-growing ornamental hot peppers are peerless for pot culture and take up far less room than their standard-sized cousins. The term "ornamental" means decorative, but not necessarily inedible. These peppers can be infernally hot and are definitely not for the faint-hearted. Try 'Pretty Purple Pepper', for its violet-colored flowers, little dark purple fruits, and compact habit. 'Starburst' produces a profusion of colorful 2-inch yellow-turning-red fruits on dwarf plants. The 1-foot-tall 'Thai Hot Ornamental' becomes covered with ½- to 1-inch upright red fruit. (Avoid purchasing *Solanum pseudocapsicum*, which produces lovely, perfectly round red fruit, resembling the edible hot pepper, to which the plant is related. It is most often called Jerusalem cherry, but is often mislabeled and sold as an ornamental pepper by careless garden centers: *It is lethally poisonous*. When in doubt, forget it.)

EGGPLANTS—Another summer vegetable favorite is eggplant, a relative of the aforementioned tomato and pepper. Try the cultivar 'Mini Bambino Hybrid', a wonderful vegetable that's truly tiny. The 14-inch plants produce copious clusters of large lavender flowers, which are followed by 1-inch dark purple fruits. Even the foliage is attractive.

LEGUMES—Lima bean 'Baby Fordhook' produces small, delicately flavored limas in 2¾-inch-long pods on amazingly compact 14-inch-tall plants. An unusual miniature bush pea is the *Fusarium*- and virus-resistant 'Micro', which bears heavy crops of small pods on leafless stems. All container-grown legumes bene-

83

The eggplant cultivar 'Mini Bambino Hybrid' makes an attractive potted plant.

fit from the addition of nitrogen-fixating rhizobacteria (naturally occurring microorganisms that form a symbiotic relationship with the legume roots they colonize). Readily available from retail seed companies, rhizobacteria are usually sold as a powder, are safe to use, and completely organic. Dust the legume seeds right before you plant them.

SQUASHES—Members of the squash family are so vigorous, they threaten to take over your garden and cover your home. But there are a number of manageable curcurbits (squash-related plants) that are worth seeking out. The cucumber cultivar 'Salad Bush' is bred especially for pot culture. It is a non-vining, disease-resistant All America Selections award winner.

Summer squash 'Sundrops Hybrid' produces beautifully shaped miniature golden squash on compact plants. Even pumpkins can be cultivated in containers! 'Baby Boo' and 'Munchkin' are two of the smallest cultivars. You can train them on any sturdy support. Try making a decorative hand-hewn trellis of grape vines, willow or hazelnut branches, or bamboo poles, for example.

BRASSICAS—Cabbage, broccoli, and their kin are notoriously space-needy, but a couple of recent introductions are quite container-worthy. Cabbage 'Gonzalez' is an early mini cabbage. The round, blue-green heads are firm and dense. Broccoli 'Munchkin' is a compact, space-saving plant with deep blue-green, full-sized heads. After harvesting, smaller-sized side-heads will appear. Don't forget to use the tougher outer foliage of broccoli in the same fashion as collard greens.

Obviously, dreams of freezers stocked with gallons of our homemade tomato sauce, ratatouille, or vegetable soup and plummeting food bills thanks to an ever-burgeoning container harvest have to remain fantasies. However, there are plenty of small, fresh, and elegant culinary avenues to explore. This recipe plays up the fresh-picked esthetics of your miniature vegetables.

> Potted vegetable plants, such as tomatoes, bell peppers,
>   hot peppers, green beans, summer squash, cucumbers,
>   peas, with ripe fruits on the plants
> Potted herbs, such as basil, chives, cilantro, and dill
> Extra-virgin olive oil
> Coarse sea salt
> Freshly cracked black pepper
> Condiments
> Bread

Timing is everything for this fun hands-on salad. The key is to clean the vegetable plants before you start—carefully wipe off the ripe fruit without dislodging it, scrub the pots, remove unsightly foliage, and clean off water spots. Place the containerized produce-laden vegetable plants on the dining table along with the potted herb plants. The idea is for the guests to pick the vegetables and herbs, dip them into the oil, salt, and pepper—and eat them with condiments, such as mixed olives, rolled anchovy fillets, capers, wedges of hard-boiled egg and crusty bread.

Clean herb and vegetable plants like this pot filled with different basils, and place them on the dining table in their containers.

CARROTS—Cultivate carrots in elongated, upright containers, to get long straight roots. Stray clay cylindrical drainage tiles filled with fertile but sandy soil are ideal for this purpose. Partially bury them in a standard pot (filled with the same sandy mixture), so they remain upright. The setup looks a little bizarre, but it is worth your time and effort. Try carrot cultivar 'Royal Chantenay'. Selection 'Thumbelina' is an easy-to-grow award winner perfect for container culture. It has round, golf ball-sized roots. Another good bet is 'Troudo Hybrid'.

OKRA—The lovely yellow, hibiscus-like flowers of okra are followed by long, horn-shaped fruit, which is integral to Cajun and African cooking. A few plants go a long way. Most okra grows several feet high, but 'Dwarf Green Longpod' can be maintained at 2½ feet.

WATERMELONS—For something completely different, plant 'Tiger Baby Icebox' watermelon. It is a semi-bush type and requires no extra staking or supporting. The 8- to 9-inch light green fruits have dark green stripes. Allow only one or two fruits per plant to ripen. Another suitable watermelon is red-fleshed 'Bush Sugar Baby', a vining cultivar that grows only 3½ feet long.

In order to harvest a tasty crop of produce, like the red cabbage and peas at left, place all vegetable pots in a spot that gets at least six hours of sun a day.

CONTAINER GARDENING TIPS

THIS SECTION IS FULL OF tips on how to grow potted plants that thrive. What growing medium you use, and how you pot a plant, water, and fertilize it, will determine the ultimate success of your potted garden. Finally, you'll learn what you can do to help your charges make it through the colder months of the year. For a map of the USDA hardiness zones, refer to page 101.

SOIL MIXES, POTTING STRATEGIES, AND OTHER CONSIDERATIONS

GARY R. KEIM

WHILE THE WORLD OF CONTAINER GARDENING affords a myriad of exciting options for growing plants, it brings new challenges, which require their own set of techniques. Once you pot a plant in a container, you have established a symbiotic relationship in which you provide food and water and the potted plant gives weeks, months, and even years of beauty in return.

SOIL CONSIDERATIONS

In nature, plants grow in soils that are complex systems of particles working as a dynamic whole. Soils are composed of sand, silt, clay, organic matter, and macro- and microorganisms. While it would seem tempting to go into the garden, scoop up some of the native soil, and pot up your plants, it is a sure-fire way to start container gardening on the wrong foot. Field soil turns rock-hard, drains poorly, and does not hold enough oxygen for container-bound plant roots.

Ask fifty gardeners what their favorite potting mix is and you are likely to get as many answers. There is no one medium that's perfect for all plants growing in containers. There are as many recipes for soil mixes as there are for chocolate chip cookies!

As long as the critical requirements of proper drainage, adequate pore space

Always choose a container that will be roomy enough for the fully grown plants.

for root aeration, water-holding ability, and plant anchoring are met, any combination of ingredients can work. Consult gardening books for various recipes that have been formulated for specific purposes and used by generations of gardeners. You'll see a wide range of ingredients in various proportions: perlite, vermiculite, pumice, sand, grit, leaf mold, compost, peat, charcoal, shredded bark, trace elements, bone meal, dried blood, lime, field soil, cottonseed meal, humus, and decomposed sod, to name the most common ones.

Lazy gardeners, like myself, can pick up pre-mixed soilless mixes at any garden center. These tend to have rather basic ingredients: peat, perlite, vermiculite, and sometimes a starter fertilizer. Mixes are useful for an extremely wide range of plants, born of the nursery industry's need to have one planting medium suitable for growing a wide variety of plants in commercial settings. Ready-made mixes drain freely, hold the proper amount of moisture, and are heavy enough to keep pots stable, yet light enough to haul around. Always moisten a premixed planting medium before you use it, to keep down dust and make it easier to handle.

CHOOSING A CONTAINER

Once you have selected a growing medium, turn your attention to the container itself. It is very important to match your plant to the proper pot size. Of course, a tiny plant can go into a small pot and move to a larger-size pot as it grows. But avoid squeezing a plant into the tightest of quarters, as it will quickly outgrow them and become a watering problem. Avoid the temptation to fill the pot up to its rim with growing mix. You need to allow space for the water to flood the soil surface and infiltrate the whole soil mass. I try to anticipate a plant's growth rate and judge from there how large a pot I want to put it in. For instance, when I install a single annual in a container, I make sure to choose a pot that is just large enough to accommodate the plant for the entire growing season. A perennial that

A teaspoon of a water-absorbing polymer before and after soaking in water. Add the expanded polymer to the potting mix and it will slowly deliver water to the plant roots as needed.

MIXING YOUR OWN—
Whatever soil mix recipe you decide to follow, make sure to blend the potting medium carefully. Never use only soil from your garden. Add the mix to the container, leaving enough room at the top so that you can flood the soil surface when watering. Wet the mix thoroughly, and you're ready to start planting.

will grow in the same container for several years requires a larger pot to begin with (at some point, however, it will need an even larger pot or root pruning.) Conversely, you can purposefully keep some plants in smaller than ideal containers to keep them small.

In recent years, English-style mixed plantings using tender perennials, and the American variation on the mixed effect using tropical plants, have been in vogue. These stunning combination plantings, often gardens in themselves, require large pots. Be sure to choose a container that's commodious enough for the fully grown plants. Achieving the full-blown, blowsy look that is the goal of these plantings requires lots of root growth.

Consider the material the container is made of. With the explosion of container gardening in the last several years, there are more containers than ever to choose from. But basically there are only two types of pots—porous and non-porous. Match the type of container to your plants' needs. Non-porous pots dry out more slowly than porous ones. They may be useful for older, possibly root-bound, plants. Some plants grow better in porous containers—Mediterranean and alpine plants, for example.

WATERING TECHNIQUES

The most critical factor in successful container gardening is watering. I have seen more container plants killed due to a lack of proper watering than anything else. Once a plant is placed in a pot of any kind, it is dependent on human intervention for water. Rain will provide some moisture, but contrary to popular belief, a shower or even a half-day soaking does not thoroughly saturate a container. However, the exact amount of water your plants will need will depend upon the weather conditions. It is best to check plants daily, even though they won't need water every day, except under extreme conditions—

intense, prolonged heat, blasting wind, or when the root system is completely pot-bound. I always keep a watering can nearby for quick touch-ups and do my thorough watering with a garden hose that's fitted with a watering wand and water breaker. It's a good idea to install a shut-off valve at the base of the watering

Keep in mind that plants will require more frequent watering as they grow. It's a good idea to check pots daily.

wand, so you can control the flow and avoid wasting water. Water thoroughly each time, until you see water running from the drainage hole. At times you may have to flood the surface of your container several times before water runs freely from the bottom. (Whatever container you choose, it is imperative that it has at least one drainage hole. Do not try to grow a plant in a container without a hole in the bottom, as it is impossible to gauge watering and you will probably drown the roots.) For tips on drought-resistant gardening in containers, see page 62.

As you observe your plants, you will begin to get a feel for those that dry out rapidly and those that stay moist longer. Keep in mind that the plants will require more frequent watering as they grow. August is a critical month; when the days shorten and the temperatures cool in autumn you can water less often.

The situations your plants grow in will affect their irrigation requirements. Containers in sites exposed to wind or those in full sun from dusk to dawn will need water more frequently than those in protected or shady areas. Use larger pots in exposed settings to provide ample growing medium, to give the plants firm anchorage, and to hold more water. Luckily, the most obvious locations for container gardens—terraces, patios, decks, pool sides, front entryways, garages—usually have easy access to water sources.

In recent years, water-absorbing polymers (hydrogels) have been developed to extend the period between waterings. These white crystal-like nuggets become transparent and gelatinous when soaked in water, acting like tiny reservoirs that deliver water to the plant roots as needed. I have used them with great success for pots in sunny, hot areas, and also for window boxes and hanging baskets. It's best to soak the polymers in a bucket before adding them to the potting mix. A handful will expand to fill the greater part of a five-gallon bucket when amply

COMPOST TEA

Compost tea is a nutrient-rich organic fertilizer that you can easily make at home. Mix one part finished compost with six parts water in a large bucket and let the mixture steep for up to a week. Then slowly pour the fluid into a second bucket or a watering can, filtering off solids with a cheese cloth, if you like. Dilute the liquid until it has a tea-like color and use it right away. If you leave the nutrient-rich tea sitting around, it will start to smell and you will have to discard it.

Apply compost tea as a liquid fertilizer for potted plants indoors or outdoors. You can also use it for foliar feeding (spraying on plant leaves). Apply the compost tea every two weeks during the growing season. When fertilizing food crops like herbs and vegetables, stop applications at least a week before harvesting. Compost and compost tea help prevent and fight fungal diseases and help keep pests at manageable levels.

The situation that your plants grow in will affect their irrigation requirements. Plants in protected, shady sites will stay moist longer.

hydrated. Allow enough time for the individual crystals to become the size of a five-cent coin, which takes approximately 20 minutes. Warm water seems to speed the process of expansion.

For large container gardens, built-in planters and large window boxes, it may be worth investing in a drip irrigation system. In such a system, plastic tubing runs from a water source to each pot, and there is a drip emitter in each pot. If the emitters run up the back of the container, the hardware usually can be discreetly hidden. These systems work with a timer or can be easily activated by turning the tap at the faucet.

FERTILIZER RECOMMENDATIONS

Container gardeners must supply not only water but also nutrients for potted plants. Most people choose liquid fertilizers, applying them while watering. You can use a pre-formulated liquid soluble fertilizer, or make compost or manure tea (see page 93 for a recipe). Serve up a dose every two weeks through the heart of the growing season, roughly from April to September. As the days shorten, you can let more time elapse between feedings. I find that heavy feeders and mixed containers need the addition of a slow-release fertilizer, such as Osmocote, to give them an extra boost. For flowering plants, I switch over to a liquid fertilizer high in phosphorus in late July to encourage more blooms in the late summer and autumn.

Containers in sites exposed to wind or those in full sun from dawn till dusk will need water more frequently. Choose drought-resistant plants for these areas.

GROOMING

Since container gardens are usually placed in prominent spots, it is necessary to groom the plants on a regular basis. Think of each container grouping as a floral arrangement that should always look fresh and colorful. For plants in the most visible locations, it is especially important to remove yellowing leaves, spent blossoms, and broken branches. Cutting off dead flowers keeps the plants from wasting energy for seed production, resulting in a prolonged floral display. When a plant dies, remove it promptly and let the surrounding specimens fill in, or plug in a new plant to keep the display lush. While grooming check for insect pests; if you spot any, deal with the situation before it gets out of hand. I find hosing plants down frequently keeps them clean. If you notice an insect outbreak, a spray of insecticidal soap will probably keep it in check.

In shady sites some plants will stretch more than they would in sun, so staking becomes an important part of maintenance. You also will find that plants grow quite rapidly at the height of the season if they are fed on a regular basis. By midsummer some of your pots may appear overgrown or shaggy. Prune growth on a regular basis to keep it compact and in scale with neighboring plants, encourage more flowering shoots, and stimulate bright, new growth on plants with colorful leaves.

Follow the above techniques and you will be well on your way to having the best container garden ever.

OVERWINTERING POTTED PLANTS

SHILA PATEL

FORTUNATE ARE GARDENERS in mild-winter regions, where container gardening is a year-round pleasure without the threat of shattered pots and frozen plants familiar to many of us. Compared with their garden-grown counterparts, container-grown plants are at a severe disadvantage when cold weather arrives. Though hardy plants have developed foliage, stems, and branches that can withstand very low temperatures, their roots are far more sensitive and vulnerable to freezing.

When planting in containers, even choosing plants hardy in your region is no guarantee that they will survive the winter. Many experts suggest that to better the odds of a plant's survival, choose one marked as hardy in two zones colder than your area. For example, if you garden in Zone 7, choose perennials, trees, and shrubs marked hardy to Zone 5 to increase the chance that the plants will survive the winter. When possible, use large containers for plants that must remain outdoors—the greater volume of soil surrounding the plants will provide increased insulation around the roots.

THINKING REGIONALLY

Luckily for gardeners in mild-winter regions (the warmer parts of Zone 8 and south), container-grown plants require little or no winterizing beyond moving pots to more sheltered locations and perhaps covering them with frost blankets when freezing temperatures are expected.

In colder regions, where freez-

Empty terra-cotta pots and store them upside down in a dry place.

Burlap screens protect evergreen woody plants against desiccating wind and sunburn.

ing temperatures are the norm at the height of winter, gardeners must protect plants from both the cold and the wind using a range of techniques. Overwintering container-grown plants outdoors is extremely challenging in the coldest regions of the country (Zone 4 and colder), where it's best to grow annuals and perennials for one short season of color.

In all but the mild-winter regions, potted plants grown on terraces and rooftops, where they will be exposed to chilling winds, should be moved to a sheltered location, such as close to a building or near a pergola or other structure, away from high winds and winter sun. When possible, group pots together, placing the most cold-sensitive plants at the center of the group, so they receive additional protection from the hardier plants.

CONTAINER CARE

The first step for winterizing the container garden is to clean and tuck away any empty pots. Store clay and terra-cotta pots upside down or on their sides in a dry place. Because they are made of porous clays, most terra-cotta pots are not suitable for leaving outside in freezing temperatures, which can cause them to crack or shatter. If you must leave terra-cotta pots outdoors, choose ones made of special clay that tolerates freezes (like Impruneta, for example). Glazed pots, which are usually fired at higher temperatures, tend to withstand freezing better than terra-cotta.

To protect planted terra-cotta and glazed containers left outdoors, wrap the sides of the pots with layers of bubble wrap or burlap covered with plastic wrap to prevent them from absorbing additional moisture once the plants go dormant and their water requirements are minimal. (Wrap pots containing evergreen plants in plastic after the first hard frost.) If you have empty concrete, cement, or clay containers that are too large to move, clean them as much as possible and cover them with lids or plastic sheeting to prevent water from collecting inside, freezing, and cracking the pots. Sturdy plastic and fiberglass pots are ideal for leaving outdoors, although some plastic pots may crack if the soil inside expands as it freezes. Wooden containers made of durable hardwoods are also suitable and will age gracefully over time.

PREPARING PLANTS FOR WINTER

Many plants prepare themselves for winter by taking cues from the environment: As days shorten and temperatures drop, many temperate plants enter the first phase of dormancy by slowing growth. To help prepare your plants for winter, stop fertilizing them by midsummer to reduce tender new growth that is vulnerable to frost, but do continue watering regularly through fall. Evergreens, especially broad-leaved evergreens, which are particularly vulnerable to desiccating winter winds, should be watered well until the first hard frost.

In fall, when nights begin to get chilly, take cuttings of tender perennials like coleus, impatiens, and geraniums to overwinter indoors. Before the first frost, move pots of annuals, tender perennials, and tropicals indoors into a bright window. Move half-hardy perennials to a cool garage or basement, where they will drop their leaves and go dormant. Cut hardy perennials that will remain outdoors back to four to five inches above the soil line once their leaves drop after the first hard frost.

Many perennials, trees, and shrubs must have a dormancy or chill period if they are to flower and fruit the following season, and cannot be moved into the house. Leave these plants outdoors and protect them using some of the techniques described in the next section. In regions with freezing winter temperatures, move them before the first hard frost to a location such an unheated garage or basement that remains about 30 to 40° F. (Although the plants will be dormant, they will benefit from some light). Reduce watering to about once a month or when

Take cuttings of tender plants when autumn evenings become chilly.

Coleus, impatiens, and geranium, shown above, are just a few of the tender perennials from which cuttings can be taken, rooted, and overwintered indoors.

soil becomes very dry; do not allow the soil to become completely dry. Plants kept in cool indoor locations tend to break dormancy earlier in the season than their outdoor counterparts; however, they should be hardened off and moved outdoors only after the danger of frost has passed.

Woody plants that must remain outdoors have a few special requirements. To prevent the branches of deciduous trees and shrubs from whipping around and breaking in winter, loosely tie branches together after the leaves have dropped. Evergreen woody plants, particularly vulnerable to desiccating winds, can be sprayed with an antidesiccant, also known as antitranspirant, and may need to be protected against harsh winter sun with burlap screens.

WINTER PROTECTION TECHNIQUES

When left outdoors, perennials, trees, and shrubs are not only subject to extreme cold and wind, but are also vulnerable to cycles of freezing and thawing that can cause heaving (plants are literally heaved out of the soil as it expands and contracts). To reduce heaving and root damage, try to re-create the naturally insulating effects of the earth. If possible, find an area in the garden that you can dig up, and sink the pots into the ground so their roots will be insulated by the surrounding soil; then mulch heavily with straw, shredded bark, or leaves as you would other plants. If this is not possible, heavily mulching container-grown plants with straw, leaves, hay, or shredded bark will provide significant protection. Some gardeners take the extra precaution of wrapping the

Top and bottom: For a beautiful display of spring flowers the next year, mulch planted containers in fall to keep them from drying out.

sides of the container with several layers of bubble wrap (to protect both delicate containers and root systems), and then mulching.

When convenient, cluster planters in a more sheltered location, such as under an eave, next to your house, or near a south-facing wall, and then mulch. Transfer small containers into a cold frame packed with sand or straw. (To create a temporary cold frame, arrange bales of hay to form four walls and top them with an old window, heavy-duty clear plastic, or a plexiglass lid.)

In open, windy areas, creating a burlap screen or windbreak provides additional protection, particularly for woody plants and shrubby perennials. Young trees and evergreen woodies, like boxwoods, which are susceptible to sunscald, will especially benefit from a burlap screen. To create a screen, pound several stakes around the plant's perimeter, and staple three-foot-wide burlap to the stakes, forming a fence around the plant. Alternatively, create a tall cage of chicken wire around the planter, and fill this with leaves or hay to provide insulation. Group smaller plants together before surrounding them with burlap or chicken wire.

The most extreme method, and one that is recommended for half-hardy plants like fuchsias and figs grown outside of their hardiness ranges, is trenching. This requires enough garden space to dig a 14- to 16-inch-deep trench, in which the plant—pot and all—can be laid down on its side and lightly re-covered with soil. The plant's branches and stems are covered with loose mulch and held in place with burlap for the season.

Regardless of which method you use, at the first signs of growth in spring, remove the heavy dressings from every planting and—if you protected them properly—you'll find them rejuvenated by their winter slumber.

USDA HARDINESS ZONE MAP

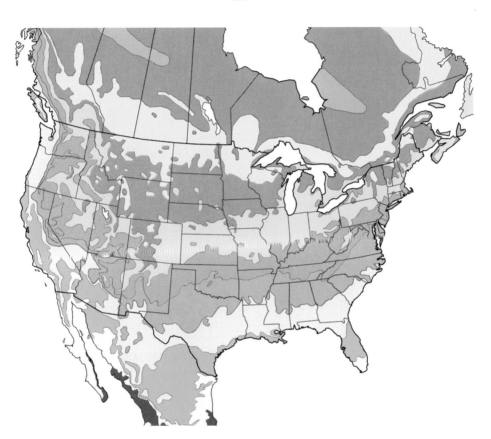

ZONES & MINIMUM WINTER TEMPERATURES (°F.)

Zone 1 below –50°	**Zone 5** –20° to 10°	**Zone 9** 20° to 30°
Zone 2 –50° to –40°	**Zone 6** –10° to 0°	**Zone 10** 30° to 40°
Zone 3 –40° to –30°	**Zone 7** 0° to 10°	**Zone 11** above 40°
Zone 4 –30° to –20°	**Zone 8** 10° to 20°	

SUPPLIERS

AQUATIC PLANTS

LILYPONS WATER GARDENS
6800 Lilypons Road, Box 10
Buckeystown, MD 21717-0010
800-999-5459
www.lilypons.com

S. SCHERER'S & SON'S
104 Waterside Road
Northport, NY 11768
631-261-7432

SLOCUM WATER GARDENS
1101 Cypress Gardens Blvd.
Winter Haven, FL 33884
863-293-7151
800-322-1896 fax
www.slocumwatergardens.com

WILLIAM TRICKER, INC.
7125 Tanglewood Drive
Independence, OH 44131
800-524-3492
216-524-6688 fax
www.tricker.com

ORNAMENTAL PLANTS

FORESTFARM
990 Tetherow Road
Williams, OR 97544
541-846-7269
541-846-6963 fax
forestfarm.com
(perennials, shrubs, trees, vines)

HERONSWOOD NURSERY
7530 NE 288th Street
Kingston, WA 98346
360-297-4172
360-297-8321
www.heronswood.com
(perennials, shrubs, trees, vines)

HIGH COUNTRY GARDENS
2902 Rufina Street
Santa Fe, NM 87505
800-925-9387
800-925-0097 fax
www.highcountrygardens.com
(drought-resistant plants, cacti,
and succulents)

PINE RIDGE GARDENS
832 Sycamore Road
London, AR 72847
501-293-4359
501-293-4659
www.pineridgegardens.com
(drought-resistant native plants)

PLANTS OF THE SOUTHWEST
Agua Fria, Route 6, Box 11A
Santa Fe, NM 87505
800-788-7333
www.plantsofthesouthwest.com
(wildflowers)

PRAIRIE NURSERY
P.O. Box 306
Westfield, WI 53964
800-476-9453
608-296-2741 fax
www.prairienursery.com
(wildflowers and native grasses)

MINIATURE VEGETABLES

THE COOK'S GARDEN
P.O. Box 5010
Hodges, SC 29653
800-457-9703
800-457-9705 fax
www.cooksgarden.com

HARRIS SEEDS
P.O. Box 24966
Rochester, NY 14624
800-514-4441
www.harrisseeds.com

J. W. JUNG SEED CO.
335 South High Street
Randolph, WI 53957
800-247-5864
www.jungseed.com

JOHNNY'S SELECTED SEEDS
310 Foss Hill Road
Albion, ME 04910
207-437-9294
www.johnnyseeds.com

TOMATO GROWERS SUPPLY CO.
P.O. Box 2237
Fort Myers, FL 33902
888-478-7333
tomatogrowers.com

UNUSUAL HERBS

THE BANANA TREE, INC.
715 Northhampton St.
Easton, PA 18042
610-253-9589
www.banana-tree.com

NICHOLS GARDEN NURSERY
1190 Old Salem Road NE
Albany, OR 97321
800-422-3985
800-231-5306 fax
www.nicholsgardennursery.com

WELL-SWEEP HERB FARM
205 Mt. Bethel Road
Port Murray, NJ 07865
908-852-5390
908-852-1649 fax
www.wellsweep.com

CONTAINERS

CLAYCRAFT PLANTERS
www.claycraft.com
(Check their website for the address
of a retailer in your area.)

FRENCH WYRES
P.O. Box 131655
Tyler, TX 75713-1655
903-561-1742
903-581-5800 fax

GARDEN SOCK
30 Blue Jay Lane
Noxon, MT 59853
800-639-9692
www.gardensock.com

GOODWIN INTERNATIONAL
3121 South Oak Street
Santa Ana, CA 92707
800-600-3200
714-241-1874 fax
www.goodwininternational.com

LUNAFORM
Cedar Lane
Sullivan, Me 04664
207-422-0923
www.lunaform.com

NICHOLS BROS. STONEWORKS
20209 Broadway
Snohomish, WA 98296
800-483-5720
www.nicholsbros.com

SEIBERT & RICE
P.O. Box 365
Short Hills, NJ 07078
973-467-8266
www.seibert-rice.com

PLANT CARE PRODUCTS

CHARLEY'S GREENHOUSE SUPPLY
17979 State Route 536
Mount Vernon, WA 98273
800-322-4707
www.charleysgreenhouse.com

GARDENER'S SUPPLY COMPANY
128 Intervale Road
Burlington, VT 05401
888-833-1412
www.gardeners.com

GARDENS ALIVE
5100 Schenley Place
Lawrenceburg, IN 47025
812-537-8650
www.gardens-alive.com

PLANT HEALTH CARE, INC.
440 William Pitt Way
Pittsburgh, PA 15238
800-421-9051

PLANT SOCIETIES

**INTERNATIONAL WATER-LILY AND
WATER GARDENING SOCIETY**
1401 Johnson Ferry Road
Suite 328-G12
Marietta, GA 30062-8115
www.iwgs.org

HERB SOCIETY OF AMERICA, INC.
9019 Chardon Road
Kirtland, OH 44060
440-256-0514

AMERICAN ROCK GARDEN SOCIETY
P.O. Box 67
Millwood, NY 10546
914-762-2948
www.nargs.org

ALPINE GARDEN SOCIETY
AGS Centre, Avon Bank, Pershore
Worcestershire, WR10 3JP
United Kingdom
www.alpinegardensociety.org

**CACTUS AND SUCCULENT SOCIETY
OF AMERICA**
1535 Reaves St.
Los Angeles, CA 90035
310-556-1923
www.cssainc.org

**THE BRITISH CACTUS &
SUCCULENT SOCIETY**
D.V. Slade
15 Brentwood Crescent
Hull Road
York, YO10 5HU
United Kingdom
www.bcss.org.uk

**DESERT PLANT SOCIETY
OF VANCOUVER**
www.cactus-mall.com/dpsv

FOR MORE INFORMATION

GARDEN ORNAMENTS
Martha Baker
Clarkson Potter Publishers
New York, 1999

GARDENING BY MAIL
Barbara J. Barton
Houghton Mifflin Company
New York, 1994

MINIATURE GARDENS
Joachim Carl
Timber Press
Portland, OR, 1990

THE COMPLETE CONTAINER GARDENER
David Joyce
The Reader's Digest Association, Inc.
Pleasantville, NY, 1996

LITTLE POTTED GARDENS
Mimi Luebbermann
Chronicle Books
San Francisco, CA, 1998

HANDBOOK ON TROUGHS
North American Rock
Gardening Society
AgPress, Manhattan, KS, 1996

BALCONIES AND ROOF GARDENS
Yvonne Rees
Ward Lock Books
London, 1992

ROOFTOP GARDENS FROM CONCEPTION TO CONSTRUCTION
Rooftop Gardens Task Force of San Francisco Beautiful
San Francisco Beautiful
San Francisco, CA, 1997

THE GARDEN DESIGN SOURCEBOOK
David Stevens
Conran Octopus
London, 1995

ROCK GARDEN PLANTS: A COLOR ENCYCLOPEDIA
Baldasarre Mineo
Timber Press
Portland, OR, 1999

NATURAL INSECT CONTROL: THE ECOLOGICAL GARDENER'S GUIDE TO FOILING PESTS
Brooklyn Botanic Garden
Brooklyn, NY, 1994

NATURAL DISEASE CONTROL: A COMMON-SENSE APPROACH TO PLANT FIRST AID
Brooklyn Botanic Garden
Brooklyn, NY, 2000

THE NATIONAL XERISCAPE COUNCIL, INC.
P.O. Box 767936
Roswell, GA 30076-7936
(A non-profit organization that serves as an informational clearinghouse for people interested in xeriscaping.)

CONTRIBUTORS

SCOTT D. APPELL has written four books, *Pansies, Lilies, Tulips,* and *Orchids.* His latest work, *A Brave New World: The Sacred Herbs of Vodou, Santeria and Candomblé,* is slated for spring 2002. In addition, he is the editor of the BBG handbook *Landscaping Indoors* (2000). He is currently director of education for the Horticultural Society of New York, a member of the Publications Committee of the Pennsylvania Horticultural Society, and a board member of the American Violet Society. He lives, writes, and teaches horticulture in New York City. His private consultation company is called *The Green Man*™.

RICHARD R. IVERSEN is a professor of ornamental horticulture at the State University of New York at Farmingdale, where he teaches courses in herbaceous plants and manages the two-acre display garden. After his return to Long Island from teaching tropical horticulture at the University of the West Indies in Barbados, he planted a tropical garden at SUNY Farmingdale. It is the subject of his recent book, *The Exotic Garden: Designing with Tropical Plants in Almost Any Climate,* Taunton Press, 1999. Iversen earned his doctoral degree at Cornell University researching the forcing requirements of herbaceous perennial plants. He is an avid collector of 19th-century decorative arts and lectures about 19th-century horticulture.

GARY R. KEIM is a freelance garden designer based near Philadelphia, with clients in the mid-Atlantic region and beyond. His designs have been featured in *Martha Stewart Living, Horticulture,* and *Fine Gardening.* He graduated from the Longwood Gardens Professional Gardener Training program in 1988. Subsequently, he worked and studied in three National Trust of England gardens; designed and maintained two horticulturally prominent private gardens in Litchfield County, CT; and was responsible for design in the famous conservatory complex at Longwood Gardens, PA. He has traveled to visit European gardens and view plants in their native habitats.

SHILA PATEL is the garden editor at marthastewart.com and the former managing editor of *National Gardening* magazine.

BILL SHANK was the cofounder (in 1984), and first president of the Horticultural Alliance of the Hamptons, in Bridgehampton, New York. He is currently vice-president/deputy garden editor of Martha Stewart Living Omnimedia, Inc. In addition, he serves both on the Garden Committee of Wave Hill and the Board of the Metro-Hort Group, based in New York City. He co-designed and maintained a much-publicized garden on eastern Long Island until 1995. He presently lives and gardens indoors in New York City.

ABBIE ZABAR is an artist, writer, and designer and has gardened in containers for over 30 years. Her first book, *The Potted Herb*, is based on her style of container gardening and is now considered the classic introduction to growing potted herbal topiaries. Her drawings are part of the permanent collection of the Hunt Institute for Botanical Documentation, one of the foremost resources for botanical art in the world.

ELLEN ZACHOS is a Harvard graduate and received her Certificate in Horticulture from The New York Botanical Garden. She specializes in tropical plants and has restored several greenhouses in the New York City area, which she now maintains for her clients. Her company, Acme Plant Stuff, installs and maintains commercial and residential interior and exterior gardens in New York City.

ILLUSTRATIONS AND PHOTOS

Window and Planter Box illustrations by **BILL SHANK**
Alpine Adventures illustrations by **ABBIE ZABAR**
DAVID CAVAGNARO cover, pages 1, 4, 23, 25, 31, 32, 39, 46, 49 top and bottom, 56, 60, 61, 63, 64, 65, 67, 68, 69, 70, 78, 79, 81, 83 left and right, 84, 98, 99
CHARLES MANN pages 5, 6, 8, 10, 13, 16, 36, 47, 66 left, 88, 92
JERRY PAVIA pages 9, 11, 20, 29, 34, 45 top, 77, 94, 95
RICHARD IVERSEN pages 18, 19
DEREK FELL pages 22, 28, 35, 37, 38, 52, 54, 59, 74, 76, 82, 86, 91 all, 96, 100 top and bottom
JOSEPH DE SCIOSE pages 24, 41
ALAN & LINDA DETRICK pages 26, 48, 57, 58, 62, 85, 97
ELLEN ZACHOS pages 40, 42, 43, 55, 71 right, 90
SUSAN GLASCOCK pages 45 bottom, 66 right, 71 left

INDEX

BROOKLYN BOTANIC GARDEN

MORE BOOKS ON

CONTAINER

GARDENING

BROOKLYN BOTANIC GARDEN
circa 1930

Brooklyn Botanic Garden is the
publisher of America's first gardening
handbooks. The series of award-winning
guides for gardeners in every region has
been published for over 55 years. Each
lavishly illustrated volume tells you how
to create a natural garden that's both
ecologically sensible and beautiful.